Jason M. Hadc   nd
writer. Jason was a Solicitor   came
a Barrister. He was the radio lawyer on LBC in London, and has
written extensively on law for magazines and newspapers. Jason
was aw   ded the MBE for his work within the law in 2012. Jason
practices law at St Ives Chambers in Birmingham.

Rhian   Davies was called to the Bar in 2001 and has more than
ten y   s' experience in family law. She regularly provides training
an   as published a number of articles within the field. She was
appointed   Deputy District Judge in 2010. Rhianon practices law at
St Ives   Chambers in Birmingham.

Also published by Constable & Robinson

Investing in Stocks and Shares

How To Make Your Own Will

Probate: the executor's guide to obtaining grant of probate and
administering the estate

HOW TO REPRESENT YOURSELF IN THE FAMILY COURT

Jason M. Hadden and Rhiannon Davies

A How To Book

ROBINSON

ROBINSON

1 3 5 7 9 8 6 4 2

First published in Great Britain in 2015 by Robinson

A CIP catalogue record for this book
is available from the British Library.

ISBN 978-1-47211-910-0 (paperback)
ISBN: 978-1-47211-911-7 (ebook)

Typeset by TW Typesetting, Plymouth, Devon
Printed and bound in Great Britain by CPI Group (UK) Ltd,
Croydon CR0 4YY

Papers used by Robinson are from well-managed forests and other responsible sources.

MIX
Paper from
responsible sources
FSC® C104740

Robinson
is an imprint of
Little, Brown Book Group
Carmelite House
50 Victoria Embankment
London EC4Y 0DZ

An Hachette UK Company
www.hachette.co.uk

www.littlebrown.co.uk

How To Books are published by Robinson, an imprint of Little, Brown Book Group. We
welcome proposals from authors who have first-hand experience of their subjects. Please set
out the aims of your book, its target market and its suggested contents in an email to Nikki.
Read@howtobooks.co.uk

Acknowledgements

The authors would like to thank Emma Kendall, Paul Ingley, Zoe Brettle and Elizabeth Craig together with the wonderful and incredibly supportive teams at How To Books and Little, Brown Book Group for their help and support, without which this book would not have been possible.

Contents

Preface

It is a sad fact that everyday relationships break down. Such breakdowns can be a bitter and painful experience for adults but where children are involved the effects can be absolutely devastating. Children can find themselves either not seeing a parent or a family member for months, or in the worst cases, even years. Where it is safe, Parliament tells us that children should be brought up having a relationship with both parents, and usually with other family members. However, there are thousands of children each year who aren't seeing a parent, grandparents or other family members.

As a result, thousands of parents are rightly bringing their disputes to Court in an attempt to have an involvement in their child's life. As Legal Aid has all but disappeared from these types of private law family disputes and lawyers' fees are often outside the ability of many people (although we are worth every penny!) we came up with the idea for this vitally important book.

This book covers what to do if you are refused the chance to spend time with your child or grandchild; and among other things, how to sort out issues of schooling, what happens if you intend to move home, change their surname or whether they be allowed to go on holiday. It also looks at Court proceedings should you be a victim of domestic violence and are seeking to prevent a violent parent from seeing their child. We explain the role of the Children and Family Courts Advisory and Support Service (CAFCASS), the National Youth Advisory Service (NYAS) and indeed the Judge. It explains the importance of mediation, completing the Court forms, witness statements and even how to draft a Court order.

This book is designed to be your friend in understanding the language and procedure of the Family Court without a lawyer. We use plain English. We keep it simple. This book is designed to help you to think about your case, what you are asking the Court to do, and to help you navigate your way through the procedural rules involved in bringing or defending a case in court and every step towards and including the final hearing. It will also help with enforcement and, if necessary, the process of appeals.

The court process can feel very alien, even scary. Our aim is to take that fear away. Bear in mind that this book can never be a complete substitute for a barrister or deal with every aspect of your particular case as the issues arise. Such a book would be impossible to write, because every single case is different. So we will tell you what should happen, and why. We don't promise to turn you into Rumpole of the Bailey or Judge Rinder; but we will give you the tools to become an effective and persuasive advocate. This is a book which can be read from cover to cover but also be dipped into as the case proceeds.

We know how important children are to everything we do. It matters. This book has been written by two dedicated family barristers with more than 30 years of experience between them, who are in Court throughout the UK arguing about family matters on a daily basis. We have taken into account everything that we have learnt and made it user friendly and easy to understand.

We hope you enjoy the book and good luck.

Jason M Hadden MBE
Rhiannon Davis
May 2015

1

The Nature of Family Disputes

Not every child is born to parents who are together, or who stay together. When relationships break down, parents have a responsibility to prioritise their children and manage their separation so as to protect them from conflict.

As adults go through the emotions around separation, this can lead to a breakdown in their communication as parents. Equally, issues such as domestic abuse can add another layer of concern and complexity.

Parents can disagree about where the children should live, how often they see the parent they do not live with and also about specific aspects of their upbringing. When parents or other family members cannot reach an agreement, either by working together or through mediation then the next alternative is through the Family Court.

It is not the role of the Family Court to decide who 'wins' or who 'loses'. Instead, the Court will conduct an inquiry into the child's welfare and reach a decision based on his or her best interests.

Remember: whether you succeed or not, at the end of your case you will still need to maintain a level of communication with the other side in order to share information about your child's welfare so that you are able to jointly take decisions about your child's upbringing where this is required by law.

The decision to take matters to court can have significant consequences for the relationship between parents. If the child or children concerned become aware of any resulting conflict between their parents, it can be harmful and upsetting for them. Parents have a duty to consider court only as a last resort and to do their best to protect their child from the consequences of their dispute. This book will help you through this process.

WHAT CAN THE FAMILY COURT RESOLVE?

The Court can only act within the scope of the law. The Family Court has three basic powers.

The Court can decide:

1. whom a child lives with;

2. how often the child sees the parent (or a family member) they do not live with;

3. decide appropriate questions about a child's upbringing. This can include questions of medical treatment and which school a child should go to.

In addition the Court can also make decisions as to whether a parent should have Parental Responsibility (sometimes abbreviated to PR) for a child.

You may already have heard terms like 'custody', 'residence' and 'contact', but these are now out of date. The time a child spends with his or her family or with whom a child lives is now set out under a 'Child Arrangements Order'.

In any legal proceedings regarding a child, the two questions you need to ask yourself first are:

Is there anything else I can do to resolve the issue first?
Mediation, negotiation and compromise can result in good outcomes in the right cases without the need for the expense, worry and possible conflict of court proceedings. Mediation is a process through which you can be helped to discuss your perspective with the other side and assisted to reach an agreement.

Am I asking for something the Court can actually order?
Be clear about what it is you want to achieve. If it is an Order that your child lives with you, or spends a certain amount of time with you, the Court can help. If it is an Order, for example, that the other parent brings up your child in exactly the same way that you do, that is less likely to be something that the Court will be able to order.

Remember
It is important to remember that the Court can impose on parents a routine for their children that neither party is wholly satisfied with. Sometimes the best and most long-lasting arrangements are ones that parents are prepared to negotiate for themselves.

2

An Introduction to the Law

This book is intended to offer you a guide to family proceedings. The law in this area can be complicated and fast moving. The aim of this section is to explain the main principles that the Court will take into account when making decisions, and also to tell you the most common parts of the law that the Court is asked to consider.

It will firstly help to explain very simply how the legal system in England and Wales works.

THE LEGAL SYSTEM
There are two different main types of law.

Acts of Parliament
Firstly, there is the law that is written down in Acts of Parliament. They are also sometimes called 'Statutes'. Statute law is the most important because it was made directly by Parliament and no Judge can make a decision, which is against an Act of Parliament. Rather, it is for Judges to interpret and apply those Acts. Acts are divided into sections and sub sections and it is normal when referring to a piece of legislation to quote the specific section you are relying on.

Case Law

The second main type of law is 'case law.' Essentially, when a Judge decides a case, they are required to deliver a judgment; this can also be called 'facts and reasons'. This judgment will need to set out not only what the decision is, but also what the facts of the case are and why the decision was made. When a judgment is given that is particularly important or interesting in terms of the way the law is applied, it will be written down and may be published. This is referred to as 'case law'.

Case law is important as it helps us understand the statute as applied by Judges.

However, every case is different, with different facts and specifics. You may be able to produce case law that suggests you should have a similar outcome, but it is not automatic that the Judge will do what you want. It is not unusual for lawyers to try to argue that particular case law does not apply because it is different from the decision the Judge has to make in their case. Case law can be found online at sites such as www.familylaw.co.uk and www.bailii.org.

Procedural Rules

In addition to the two main types of law explained above there are also Procedural Rules. These rules are written down and also approved by Parliament in some form. They are not the same as Acts of Parliament or case law but they are important rules, which need to be complied with. The main rules you will need to deal with are the Family Procedure Rules 2010. These will help you with the procedure, including the types of hearings there will be and the time limits the Court will expect you to comply with when taking certain steps.

The Children Act 1989 is the principal statute that Judges will apply when deciding applications about children. This tells them what things to take into account when making their decision and also sets out the Orders they can make.

Section 1 of The Children Act 1989 sets out some of the principles the Court will use to make a decision. Other important sections are at Section 8 (the types of Orders the Court can make), Section 10 (provisions about who can apply for Orders about a child) and Section 11 (enforcing and monitoring contact).

Child Arrangements Orders are the Orders that set out whom a child will live with, and when and how they will spend time with parents or other relatives.

A Specific Issue Order can require a person, usually a parent, to do something in relation to a child, and a Prohibited Steps Order can require a person not to do something in relation to a child. These Orders are allowed under Section 8 of the Children Act 1989.

Prohibited Steps Orders, Specific Issue Orders and Child Arrangements Orders can also be called Section 8 Orders after the section of the Children Act they are based on.

The Children Act 1989 has been changed since the day it was first written. Later laws, such as the Child and Families Act 2014, have amended it but it is still referred to as the Children Act 1989. It is therefore important when you are looking into the law that you make sure you are looking at the up-to-date version.

A WORD ABOUT HUMAN RIGHTS

Whenever the Court makes a decision about the upbringing of a child, it is interfering in a family's personal and private life. The Court is required to act in the best interests of the child and there are many occasions when the Court makes an Order to make things better for the child.

The Human Rights Act 1998

The Human Rights Act 1998 is an Act of Parliament which had the effect of requiring the Court to make decisions that are consistent with the parties' human rights. Our rights are set out in the European Convention on Human Rights, which are included in the Human Rights Act. The main human rights we think about in family law are set out in Article 6 and Article 8. Article 6 is the right to a fair trial and Article 8 is the right to a private and family life.

Where the rights of a child and a parent conflict, the rights of the child prevail. Just by way of example, in the case of a violent parent, the child has a right to be kept safe and not be exposed to harm. By the same token, the violent parent would argue that he or she should have direct contact with the child because they have a right to a family life including their children. The Court has to consider both sets of rights, and clearly there can be no middle ground in some of the issues that arise. The Court is obliged to place greater weight on the rights of the child.

THE MAIN LEGAL PRINCIPLES IN THE CHILDREN ACT 1989

The Court will make its decision based on specific legal principles and these are contained in the Children Act 1989.

The Welfare Principle

Firstly, we have the 'Welfare Principle' which is applied whenever the Court has to decide a question relating to the upbringing of a child. The Welfare Principle is very simply that the child's welfare in such cases shall be the Court's paramount consideration. It is Section 1(1) of the Children Act 1989.

The 'Delay' Principle

In addition, the Court also has to take into account at Section 1(2) the general principle that any delay in dealing with the proceedings is likely to be detrimental to the welfare of the child. This is an important section that can be relevant when; for example, the Court is asked to adjourn a case.

Ongoing parental involvement

Whenever the Court is thinking about making, ending or varying a Child Arrangements Order, or another Order under Section 8 (or making an Order called a Special Guardianship Order – see page 66), the Judge must also presume, unless the contrary is shown, that the involvement of the parent in the life of the child concerned will further the child's welfare.

It is also the case that any decision by the Court represents the State getting involved in the private life of families. For this reason, Judges need to think carefully before making Orders and do not go further than is necessary.

'No Order' Principle

Section 1(5) requires the Court not to make an Order unless to do so it is better for the child than to make no Order at all. You may need to justify to the Court why you should have a Court Order for your time with your children rather than rely on a simple agreement that has been reached in negotiations.

THE WELFARE 'CHECKLIST'

Whenever the Court is thinking about making, ending or varying a Child Arrangements Order, or another Order under Section 8, there is a checklist of things to be considered. The items on the Welfare Checklist are:

1. the ascertainable wishes and feelings of the child concerned (considered in the light of his age and understanding);

2. his physical, emotional and educational needs;

3. the likely effect on him of any change in his circumstances;

4. his age, sex, background and any characteristics of his that the Court considers relevant;

5. any harm that he has suffered or is at risk of suffering;

6. how capable each of his parents, and any other person in relation to whom the Court considers the question to be relevant, is of meeting his needs;

7. the range of powers available to the Court under this Act in the proceedings in question.

You will often see this checklist set out in court papers. In particular, it is often an important part of CAFCASS or other welfare reports (see Chapter 12).

Some points on the Welfare Checklist

Firstly, the Welfare Checklist does not apply to every decision of the Court. It does not apply, for example, when you are asking the Court to give you permission to make an application.

Secondly, the items listed in the checklist are listed in no particular order of priority. It is not the case that one item is more important than any other, although it is fair to say that some aspects of the checklist may be more relevant than others to your particular situation.

Thirdly, in any application you make to the Court where the Welfare Checklist applies you should always apply the Welfare Checklist in your application and arguments to the Court.

Understanding the Welfare Checklist

Some of the items on the checklist require further explanation:

> *(The ascertainable wishes and feelings of the child concerned (considered in the light of his age and understanding)'*

The wishes and feelings of the child are obviously very important; however, this does not mean in every case that the child will automatically be given the result that they may say they want.

There is no 'magic age' after which a child who is still young enough to be covered by the Children Act must be listened to and their direct wishes acted upon. It is more correct to say that the older the child and the more considered the child's wishes, the less likely it is that the child will not be listened to. Much of this will depend on the decision being made. If an older child expresses a wish to live with a parent who poses a direct and serious risk, for example, it is more likely that the Court will not decide the case based on that child's wishes and feelings but be guided by all of the evidence in the case.

'The likely effect on him of any change in circumstances'

The status quo is important. If the child's needs are being met by a particular set of arrangements, then evidence will need to be brought to prove that change will be in that child's best interests. This does not mean that the status quo is never changed but the Court is likely to require good reason to make big changes, such as a change of the child's main carer, where that carer is not meeting the child's needs.

'Any harm the child has suffered or is at risk of suffering'

This harm can be emotional or physical and can include neglect. It is important to note that this includes the risk of future harm. The denial of a relationship with a parent can be considered 'harm' under this section, unless, for example, contact has been stopped or limited due to proven welfare concerns.

There is no rule in law, or reference in the 'checklist' that states that children should live with their mother rather than their father; nor that one particular pattern of contact must apply in all cases.

THE OVERRIDING OBJECTIVE

In addition to the Children Act 1989, the Court also needs to have regard to the Family Procedure Rules and, in particular, the 'Overriding Objective' when exercising its powers under the Rules. This covers many types of case management decision including the type of evidence it will allow and whether an expert report is needed (see Chapter 13).

The Overriding Objective is contained at paragraph 1.1 of the Family Procedure Rules and reads as follows:

1. These rules are a new procedural code with the overriding objective of enabling the Court to deal with cases justly, having regard to any welfare issues involved.

2. Dealing with a case justly includes, so far as is practicable:

   (a) ensuring that it is dealt with expeditiously and fairly;

   (b) dealing with the case in ways that are proportionate to the nature, importance and complexity of the issues;

   (c) ensuring that the parties are on an equal footing;

   (d) saving expense; and

   (e) allotting to it an appropriate share of the Court's resources, while taking into account the need to allot resources to other cases.

The Overriding Objective is quite straightforward and allows the Court to manage its cases based on the factors set out above.

PRIVACY IN FAMILY PROCEEDINGS

Once court proceedings begin, you need to remember that court hearings will take place in private and there are limits on the number of people who may see the court papers.

If you breach those limits, you will be breaking the law and may face sanctions from the Court.

To be completely safe, you are advised to avoid discussing the court proceedings with anyone. *Do not* talk about the case on social media. It is not unusual for evidence from social media, such as Facebook or Twitter to be produced in family cases and you could damage your case, even unintentionally.

3

Applying for a Child Arrangements Order

A Child Arrangements Order is an Order from the Court that states whom a child lives with and with whom they spend time and for how long. From 22 April 2014, Child Arrangement Orders replaced 'Residence Orders' and 'Contact Orders' under Section 8 of the Children Act 1989.

The government brought about the changes as it was becoming concerned that some parents were arguing more about the labels and status that attached to such Orders ('Residence' and 'Contact') rather than actually putting the needs and interests of their children first.

As such they sought to bring about a sea change in children law, reiterating that the priority should be that the interests of the child are the paramount consideration.

The new system for dealing with applications made by parents about their child is set out in the Family Procedure Rules as the Child Arrangements Programme. It is worth reading this document in addition to this book, as it will show you the rules that the Court

will apply. It can be found at: www.justice.gov.uk/downloads/
family-justice-reform/pd-12b-cap.pdf

The Court considers that parents with Parental Responsibility
should try to work things out between themselves rather than
resorting to court proceedings. At the forefront of this change
is mediation and the intention that parents, or those people with
Parental Responsibility, should come to court only as a last
resort. Families are encouraged to use dispute resolution services,
including mediation, as alternatives to court proceedings.

Applicants are required to attend a Mediation Information and
Assessment Meeting (MIAM) prior to making an application to the
Court for a Child Arrangements Order unless an exemption applies.
Legal aid was removed from private law children proceedings in all
but the most extreme cases. As such, if resolution cannot be reached
by way of agreement or mediation, then the Court will decide. The
court proceedings follow a particular order (unless there is a reason
to change it). This is as follows:

◆ The making of the Application

◆ CAFCASS Safeguarding checks

◆ First Hearing/Dispute Resolution Hearing

◆ Finding-of-fact Hearing (if necessary)

◆ Dispute Resolution Hearing

◆ Further Case Management Directions (if necessary)

◆ Final Hearing

The Family Procedure Rules set all this out in a helpful flowchart, which is reproduced in Appendix 2 of this book.

A Child Arrangements Order can state:

> 'with whom a child is to live, spend time or otherwise have contact, and

> when a child is to live, spend time or otherwise have contact with any person.'

It will therefore set out whom a child can live with and it should also set out when the child sees the parent he or she does not live with.

ATTENDING A MEDIATION INFORMATION ASSESSMENT MEETING (MIAM)

Before an application can be made to court, you are now required to prove that you have attended a Mediation Information Assessment Meeting (MIAM). You will need a form FM1 (Family Mediation 1) to show the Court that you have been to a MIAM when you start court proceedings.

The purpose of mediation is to see if court proceedings can be avoided and that a negotiated agreement about the child can be reached between the parties. However, mediation only really works if parties are prepared to compromise. You need to go in with an open mind and be prepared to listen to the points that are made, but also to explain what is important to you and why.

Courts are required to know that mediation has been considered before they are able to proceed with your application.

The Mediation Information Assessment Meeting normally takes between 45 minutes to an hour and is attended by you and a mediator to see if there are alternative ways to find a resolution to the child dispute.

The mediator will explain to you:

- what your options might be;

- what mediation is, and how it works;

- the benefits of mediation and other appropriate forms of resolving disputes;

- the likely costs of using mediation;

- if you are eligible for free mediation and Legal Aid.

The meeting can be between the mediator and just you, or with your ex-partner too.

You may be eligible for Legal Aid to cover the cost. But if not, you will be advised of the cost, which will usually be about £150, plus VAT, for each of you.

What happens after the meeting?

The mediator will be able to tell you after the meeting whether your case is suitable for mediation. If it is, he or she will advise you of the next steps.

What happens if mediation does not go ahead?

If, after your MIAM, it is considered that mediation is not suitable in your case, the mediator will supply you with a FM1 form, which they will sign. This form confirms that you have attended an MIAM. The Court will then allow you to issue proceedings.

It is important that people taking part in mediation are able to speak freely. For this reason, what you say in mediation in relation to what you would accept as part of negotiations is not to be repeated in court. The discussions in mediation are protected.

Your FM1 form will allow you to start court proceedings in the following 4 months. If you wait longer than this, you will have to go through the process again to see if mediation is now possible.

Exceptions to attending an MIAM

There are exceptions to the need to attend a MIAM; these are:

◆ Where an emergency application is being made to the Court

◆ On applications to the Court without notice

◆ Enforcement of a Court Order

◆ Consent applications

◆ Applications in ongoing proceedings

◆ Where there has been domestic abuse or an allegation of domestic abuse (by either you or the other party) in the last 12 months resulting in a Police investigation

◆ Where there are financial difficulties and one of you is bankrupt

◆ You do not know how to contact the other person

◆ There are child protection issues and Social Services have been involved

◆ Where you cannot find any mediator within 15 miles of your home who can see you for a MIAM within 15 working days. You have to show that you have contacted at least 3 mediators

◆ You have an FM1 form that is less than 4 months old

UNDERSTANDING SHARED CARE

It is also the case that a child can live with more than one person.

For instance, a child may live with the mother for four days in a week and the father for three days or vice versa. This shared arrangement is becoming more common. It does not, however, mean that a child must spend 50 per cent of the time with each parent. This is often referred to as a 'shared care' arrangement and used to be referred to as a 'shared residence' agreement. It basically means that a child can have two homes.

A Child Arrangements Order setting out with whom a child will live can also be made in favour of people who do not hold Parental Responsibility. Where this happens that person will automatically gain Parental Responsibility for the duration of the Child Arrangements Order.

In many cases, even after court proceedings have been issued, parents will agree the arrangement for their children and the Court will not need to make any Order.

UNDERSTANDING THE CHILD ARRANGEMENTS ORDER

How long does a final Child Arrangements Order last?

A final Child Arrangements Order lasts until a child is 18 years old unless the Court prior to this date ends it.

What if there is already a Residence Order or Contact Order in place?

If you currently have a 'Residence Order' or 'Contact Order' made under the 'old' law, do not worry – you do not need to do anything.

That Order is still valid and enforceable. It does not need to be converted into a Child Arrangements Order. As of 22 April 2014 a 'Residence Order' and/or a 'Contact Order' automatically became a Child Arrangements Order so there is no need to bring the matter back to court.

If, however, there is an Order in place and you want it to be changed in some way, then you can apply to the Court to vary the Order. This is done in the same way as making a fresh application. You use the same forms to start the proceedings and the Court will follow the same process.

What happens if the Child Arrangement Order is breached?

Should a party fail or refuse to comply with a Child Arrangement Order, an application can be made to the Court to enforce the Order (see Chapter 18).

What are 'residence' and 'contact'?

The Court can make an Order for you to be able to spend time with your child. Although 'Residence' and 'Contact' Orders have been replaced by Child Arrangements Orders, sometimes the terms 'Residence' and 'Contact' are used in discussions at court to describe the ways in which the Court can decide a child should see their parents.

'Residence' can be used to refer to the person or home a child shall live in. 'Contact' can be used to refer to the time the child spends with the parent they do not live with.

When you apply for a Child Arrangements Order, you need to think about the sort of time you want to spend with your child.

Spending time with a child

It is important to actually give some thought at the outset and also prior to speaking with CAFCASS or any court hearings (including the Final Hearing) as to what amount of time you want to spend with your child, particularly if it is not feasible or possible for the child to live with you.

Be realistic. Your starting point may well be that you want to spend every moment with your child, including after school, every weekend and every holiday.

While that may seem like a good idea, have you actually considered your other commitments such as friends, family (any other children you see regularly), work and new partners, which may impact upon the time you actually have available to spend with your child?

The biggest commitment is usually work. Most people only have between 20–25 days holiday a year. In addition, these days we spend a lot of time working outside of the more conventional 9 a.m. to 5 p.m., for example if you undertake shift work.

Children at school age have a lot more holiday than adults. If your starting point is that you want to see the children all of the time or perhaps share holidays with the other parent, is that really practical?

Children usually have two weeks holiday at both Christmas and Easter and six weeks holiday on average in the summer. With additional half-term holidays of three weeks, in total your child is actually on holiday from school for approximately thirteen weeks every year.

Taking this factor into account you may consider it more reasonable to negotiate and ask the Court for perhaps two weeks in the summer, one week at Christmas and a few days at Easter and the half-term holidays. You should think about this before you turn up at court. Be clear in your mind what you are asking for and that it is manageable.

What about Father's Day and Mother's Day? Both are Sundays. Are these important days when you would wish to spend time with the child?

The date of your birthday? The child's birthday? It is also common for both parents to want to share some of this time with their child. Is there a party planned? How will this impact on the child's birthday? It is not always possible, particularly when the child is still at school, to see the absent parent. So it may be that agreement can be reached with respect to the day before or the day after the birthday. Any other children's birthdays? Do you want your child to attend the birthday of a sibling?

Give consideration to other days of celebration where appropriate, such as during Ramadan and Diwali. Are there any other family weddings or celebrations? It is better to try to be as clear as possible about what time you want to spend with the child.

How do I resolve the issue of Christmas?
The most contentious day of the year for many parents when it comes to disputes over time spent with a child is, of course, Christmas. There are no hard and fast rules in law or from the Courts with regard to contact at Christmas. There is also no expectation that because a child resides with one parent it means

that they have the child live with them every Christmas. It is most common that a child will spend either a portion of each Christmas Day with each parent or have alternate Christmas Days with a parent.

There appear to be two main approaches to Christmas that the Courts may take.

The first is that one parent has the whole of Christmas Day one year and the other parent has the whole of Christmas Day the following year. The advantages of this would be that the child gets in fact, two full Christmas Days over the Christmas period, with one parent on Christmas Day and the other parent later during the Christmas period. The other advantage of this arrangement is where the parents no longer live near to one another or now have other Christmas commitments, such as perhaps a second family. It could be drafted like this:

> *'the child [name] shall spend from 6 p.m. on 24 December until 11 a.m. on 26 December with the mother and the child spend from 11 a.m. on 26 December until 6 p.m. on 28 December with the father in even years (by way of example 2016, 2018, 2020)'*

> *'the child [name] shall spend from 6 p.m. on 24 December until 11 a.m. on 26 December with the father and the child spend from 11 a.m. on 26 December until 6 p.m. on 28 December with the father in odd years (by way of example 2015, 2017, 2019)'*

The second approach is to split Christmas Day in two – whereby one party has the first half of the day and this will of course include

Christmas Eve until, say, 12 noon on Christmas Day and the other parent has the afternoon and early evening until perhaps Boxing Day.

It could be drafted like this:

> *'the child [name] shall spend from 6 p.m. on 24 December until 12 noon on 25 December with the father and from 12 noon on 25 December until 6 p.m. on 26 December with the mother and this will apply each year commencing in xxxx'*

There is no set rule and these suggestions are provided just by way of a guide to assist in your considerations. It will always be better to try to agree, where possible, Christmas arrangements with the other parent. It is much better than have the Court try to determine an outcome which may not suit either of you.

Spending regular time with your child

There is also the question of how much regular time you may wish to spend with your child. Where there is overnight contact it is not unusual for the child to live with one parent for one or two nights (it can be longer) every weekend or every alternate weekend. It is becoming more common that Courts prefer the option of every alternate weekend rather than weekly as this allows the child some space to do their own thing but also allows each parent a full weekend with the child.

Consideration may also be given to the non-resident parent to having dinner once (again it can be more often) a week after school.

In addition, consideration can also be given to either telephone calls or Skype/FaceTime conversation with the child each week.

When it comes to this level of minutiae it is about maintaining a relationship with the child which is both child focused and manageable. The last thing anyone would want is for the child to be let down after a parent agrees a schedule because the schedule is in fact either unrealistic or unworkable for the parent.

Being realistic

So be realistic. Be flexible but ensure that you have set out prior to the Final Hearing, and ideally in your witness statement, what level of time you would wish to spend with the child. The last thing the Court would expect to hear is that you have not given any consideration to this question. Have it worked out in advance and written out so that it is clear. It can be very helpful to bring a diary or a calendar with you to court (many phones these days have calendar apps on them – but do make sure that you turn a phone to 'silent' mode in the courtroom) so that you can visualise what days you are proposing to spend with the child.

It should be pointed out that in the court process these negotiations can get quite fraught with you and the other side arguing over an hour here or there. So be prepared to negotiate and be sensible as this is ultimately about the child.

Flexibility

The Court can also allow for there to be flexibility in the Court Order and the normal phrase, which the Court adopts, is:

> *'whatever additional contact (or time spent) as can be agreed between the parties'*

This is because it is incredibly difficult to be so prescriptive about where and what a child will do for the rest of their childhood. The Court will expect a degree of flexibility between parents.

When the child lives with you

Obviously the same principles apply if the child lives with you and you are the respondent to the other party's application. Give consideration in advance to what the other party's proposals are to spend time with the child. Are there any commitments that the child has to school, after-school clubs or any other activities, which prevent the child seeing the other parent on that specific day? What is the situation with homework? Does this have to be done with you or can all or part of it be undertaken when in the care of the other parent?

If you have letters or leaflets which confirm the child's activities on a specific day, then these are documents which could be attached as exhibits to your witness statement.

Again, work out in advance what you consider appropriate prior to responding to the other party, speaking with CAFCASS or prior to any court hearing.

Supervised contact

Supervised contact is often the first type of contact to be offered to a parent where there are issues of domestic abuse or when there has been a gap in time between the child seeing the person seeking to spend time with them.

It allows the child to spend time with their parent but with someone else there, who is considered appropriate to ensure that the child is safe.

Contact Centres

It is important firstly to be clear about what this involves. 'Supervised' contact is used to describe contact that is formally monitored. This can be through professionals at a 'contact centre' or by a mutually agreed third party such as another friend or relative.

'Supported' contact is used to describe contact that still has another party present but the level of monitoring is less than it would be for supervised. This would usually be where there are no risks involved with the person seeking to have contact, but perhaps they have not seen the child for a while or the child is a baby and they do not have any or much experience with children of that age.

Contact centres can be a useful resource. The idea of having supervised time with your child can be unappealing, especially when you feel you have done nothing wrong and should be having unsupervised time. However, if you are in the process of applying for a Child Arrangements Order and the CAFCASS report or Final Hearing is several weeks away, it can be worth considering seeing the child in a contact centre just to build up the relationship with them. This contact is normally weekly or fortnightly and for between one or two hours a time. There is normally a fee although in certain circumstances this can and will be funded by CAFCASS.

The Court is not going to assume you have done anything wrong if you choose to accept supervised contact rather than wait for weeks or months without seeing your child. Having a regular contact arrangement in place, even supervised or supported, can give CAFCASS something to assess, rather than having a long gap in contact and a process of reintroduction.

One of the advantages of a contact centre is that some centres can offer reports of the supervised contact they have seen. These centres and services are not cheap, but if you can afford them, you will be able to build up a record of your time with your child. If your contact is of good quality, this can provide useful evidence for any future hearing.

Make sure when you are looking at contact centres that you check what sort of contact they are offering. Supervised contact is usually used to describe time observed on a one-to-one basis. Supported contact is usually used to describe time that is less strictly observed.

There are usually toys and resources in the contact centre that you can use but you can bring your own. It is always worth checking in advance if there are any rules about this. If you are able to, try to find out from the resident parent bringing the child whether you are to give any food or drinks, and if so what your child enjoys.

Contact centres are a good way to allow the child to be handed over to the other parent without the need for a face-to-face meeting, which can be difficult. Contact centre staff should be able to provide advice and reassurance to both parents and to monitor the child's well-being.

It is not common for the resident parent to stay and 'monitor' contact, save for the handover. Contact should be for the non-resident parent and child to enjoy. Where other family members also want to see the child at this contact then this can be agreed, although the priority is usually to build or rebuild a relationship between the child and the non-resident parent.

DEALING WITH HANDOVER

One area of dispute between parties is how and where the child will be 'handed' over to the other. Where the parties do not get on with one another and this can prove distressing for the child, then it is often unhelpful for them to both attend handover. One solution is for an appropriate family member to undertake the handover with the other parent. Another option is to locate a safe venue, such as outside a Police Station or public place (with CCTV).

Where there are no issues between the parents then the child will usually be picked up at either parent's home or the school. Where there is a distance between the two homes then it could be agreed that one party would collect the child and the other at the end of contact would come and return the child. The other option is, of course, to meet halfway. Again, there is no hard and fast rule from the Court, but an expectation of flexibility and being sensible by putting the child's welfare first.

COURT ORDERS

Whenever the Court makes a decision, whether that is a Child Arrangements Order or directions to set up a Final Hearing, that decision is recorded in an Order. It's not unusual in cases where one party is represented for the Judge to ask the legal representative to write the Order. The Court will expect the Order to set out what has been ordered, and for you to try to agree the wording with the other side.

If there are disagreements about how the Order is worded, the Court can be asked to decide them. You should also be given a copy of any completed Order to take away with you, if possible. If this doesn't happen, then you will need to make sure the Court has the correct address for you because one will be posted out. Be aware that this can take a few days to be done.

If neither side is represented, you could be asked to write the Order. The Ministry of Justice has provided set forms for Court Orders, which must be used, whether you are a lawyer or not. Copies of these forms of Order can be found in Appendix 1.

The forms may look quite complicated but they are designed so that they contain lots of information about what each person asked for at the hearing and any agreements that were reached.

When filling in the forms you are asked to comment on things such as the 'Timetable for the Child'. What this does is ask you to think about any important dates for your child that are coming up. If, for example, your child is about to start school, it is relevant to put that down, as this will have an effect on how often the child is available to spend time with you.

The Orders also refer to 'recitals' and 'undertakings'. Recitals are agreements or other important things that need to be written down but are not important enough to be part of the Order. This may include things such as if you agree that you will use a notebook to communicate with the other parent (called a 'communications book' with the idea that it is taken to contact and messages are written about the child's welfare).

Undertakings are more formal than that. This is where a parent promises to the Court that they will do something, or will not do something. Examples may include undertaking not to drink alcohol during the time you spend with the child. Undertakings can have

Notices called 'Penal Notices' attached to them, which means you can be punished by a fine or imprisonment if you breach them, so always be clear when an undertaking is mentioned whether they will have a Penal Notice attached.

The draft Orders are referred to by number and the letters CAP. CAP refers to the Child Arrangements Programme, which is the main set of rules that governs these types of proceedings. A copy of the precedent CAP form can be found in Appendix 1.

CAP1 is the Order the Court makes when your case is first started and is often done without a hearing. It is used to set out the time and date of the hearing and any steps to be taken before then.

CAP2 is to be filled out after the First Hearing and Directions Appointment and is used to set out what was agreed at that hearing, including directions for any reports.

CAP2L is a shorter version of CAP2, which can also be used for the First Hearing and Directions Appointment, and any other short Directions Hearing after that.

CAP3 is the Order made at the Dispute Resolution Appointment.

CAP4 is the form used when the Court is making a Final Order.

The Role of Legal Representation

The role of a lawyer is to help you put your case to the Court and to give you legal advice at every stage of the process. This means drafting the application, assisting you to prepare witness statements and speaking for you in court. They will liaise with the Court and the other parties on your behalf and will ensure that you comply with legal requirements. They can advise you on how best to run your case, the likely outcome and whether you have grounds for appeal in the event that your application or position does not succeed.

While this book is a general guide, it is not a substitute for having a lawyer who can assist you in navigating court proceedings.

Cases involving children can be particularly sensitive. A good lawyer will be able to draw on their own experiences of other cases to assist clients. This is experience you will not have.

The cost of a lawyer is obviously a consideration when deciding whether or not to seek legal representation. It is not cheap. The reason it is not cheap is because it is a service that can only be provided by people who have been properly trained and who are qualified. Lawyers are also regulated by their professional body and must have valid insurance in place in order to practise. The outcome of the application relating to your child is something you are likely to have to live with for many years to come. This is a particular concern if you do not get the result you want or even a result that you can tolerate. For this reason, you should think carefully about whether to instruct a lawyer to assist you. Legal advice can seem expensive but it is on the whole a worthwhile investment. It really comes down to what you value most in life.

So when deciding whether or not to instruct a lawyer, a good rule of thumb is to consider how important getting the right result is to you and whether or not you can live with a less favourable outcome.

WHAT DOES IT MEAN TO REPRESENT YOURSELF?

The purpose of this book is to put you in the best possible position to represent yourself by setting out the process the Court will follow. If you have read it, you will be in a much better position than most other litigants in person. However, there is no substitute for a Solicitor or Barrister who is legally qualified and who can provide you with advice and representation. Your case will have its own individual facts and issues and this is not something this book can take into account.

If you represent yourself you will need to:

- understand the issues in the case and how best to set out your case;

◆ deal with legal requirements such as how to draft your application/respond to the application, set out your witness statement, filing and serving;

◆ liaise with the Court and the other side to comply with directions, negotiate extensions and generally assist the progression of the case. This may be liaison directly with your ex-partner if they are also unrepresented or with their lawyers;

◆ consider what witnesses to call to give evidence, how to present their evidence to the Court and how to get them to court;

◆ respond to potentially serious allegations, such as domestic abuse, abuse or mistreatment of children, alcohol/drug use, etc., which can have an effect on your future care of or contact with your children or any future children you might have;

◆ consider what evidence you need to substantiate your case, such as drugs/alcohol testing, Police records, phone records, medical records, etc.;

◆ speak in court – both dealing with things such as what directions are needed to bring the case to its conclusion and at the Final Hearing when you will have to explain your case to the Court in detail and question the other side, any witnesses they might have and any experts, such as CAFCASS;

◆ be questioned by the other side with no one else to speak up or object on your behalf.

INSTRUCTING A LAWYER

When taking the step to see a Solicitor, you may wish to enquire as to whether they have a particular expertise in family law or are accredited in Children Law by the Law Society. The other concern is obviously their fees. It will ease your mind to know that there are many options available and firms are taking a more flexible approach due to the current competitive market.

Solicitors have different ways of charging clients and methods of charging may vary. For example, firms may offer a fixed-fee arrangement, charge by an hourly rate or offer a 'pay as you go' service.

OBTAINING FREE LEGAL ADVICE

There are ways to get free legal advice. There are certain charities that provide some free legal advice to people who cannot afford to pay for a Solicitor and those for whom Legal Aid is not available.

The Citizens Advice Bureau and your local Law Centre may be able to assist you.

Some Solicitors may offer up to an hour's free legal advice or a free initial appointment for an allotted time. They will give you an idea of the likely costs and your prospects of success. It may also be it gives you sufficient information to proceed with your case without further representation.

APPLYING FOR LEGAL AID

Legal Aid means that the State will pay for all or some of the costs of your legal representation.

Legal Aid is not readily available for all matters and a strict eligibility criterion applies. Not every law firm offers Legal Aid as Legal Aid can only be provided by an organisation with a contract with the Legal Aid Agency. The criteria for Legal Aid includes financial eligibility and also factors such as the merits of your case, and whether you have been a victim of domestic violence.

There are different types of Legal Aid and different levels of representation from general advice to representation at court.

There are online tools that will assist you in finding out if you are eligible for Legal Aid, the level of Legal Aid you are entitled to and whether you are required to pay a contribution. You should contact the Community Legal Advice helpline on 0345 345 4345 or a Solicitor dealing in Legal Aid who can assess your eligibility.

FIXED FEE

Fixed Fees are popular and help peace of mind, as there are no hidden charges.

Fixed Fees are agreed prior to the start of a case and are fixed irrespective of the eventual actual costs incurred on your case. This is reassuring, as regardless of how much work is undertaken on your case, you will only pay the agreed Fixed Fee.

A Fixed Fee can be agreed for a single appointment or for the whole matter.

PAYING PRIVATELY – HOURLY RATES

The Hourly Rate of a Solicitor may vary and a number of factors such as seniority and expertise will impact on this rate.

Hourly Rates usually start at approximately £100 plus VAT per hour for junior/newly qualified staff. A senior Solicitor usually charges at rates in the region of £200 plus VAT per hour. The location of the law firm may also impact upon rates as city centre firms may charge more.

Your Solicitor should give you an estimate of how long the matter shall last and an estimate of the likely costs you are expected to pay. You should receive regular updates by way of a bill of costs setting out the amount of work undertaken on your file, and the amount owing on your account.

PAY AS YOU GO

'Pay As You Go' is a new approach and not all law firms offer this service.

Under the Pay As You Go approach you manage the day-to-day running of your matter from start to finish but with help from your Solicitor being available.

The aim is that you remain in control as you only pay for advice as and when you require it. This approach also means that there are no unexpected charges or bills.

DIRECT/PUBLIC ACCESS WORK

You are now able to access a Barrister directly without having to involve a Solicitor.

This is becoming very popular as by going directly to a Barrister you avoid paying the additional fees involved in instructing a Solicitor.

A Barrister can provide advice, draft documents and represent you in court.

There are, however, some limits on the work a Barrister can do, therefore there may be some situations where you require a Solicitor as well.

Not all Barristers accept direct access work, therefore enquiries will need to be made with their Clerks at Chambers, who will be able to assist.

You can find Barristers who specialise in family proceedings by using the Internet. Barristers are self-employed but are part of Chambers. Their profiles and areas of expertise should be set out on their Chambers' website. Personal recommendations are also a good way to find a Barrister.

MCKENZIE FRIENDS

A McKenzie Friend is a lay person who can accompany you at court and assist you. It is very unlikely that a family member will be allowed to act in this capacity. They can help you in organising your documents, take notes and make suggestions as to what questions you might want to ask a witness. However, they have no right to address the Court and are usually not legally qualified. They are not usually covered by insurance and are not regulated by a professional body.

If you do want someone to act as a McKenzie Friend, you should tell the Court this at the earliest opportunity as you will need the permission of the Court. In most cases you will be allowed the assistance of a McKenzie Friend but not all. It is helpful if you can explain to the Court why you are asking for a McKenzie Friend, whom in particular you are asking for and provide a copy of their CV if possible. You may be unfamiliar with court proceedings and struggle to understand what is going on during a court hearing. The proposed McKenzie Friend may have experience of helping people in similar circumstances. It is important that the McKenzie Friend understands that their role is to assist you, rather than to act as your lawyer. They cannot act as your advocate in court (unless the Judge specifically allows them) but merely advise you in what to say. It is also important that they understand the rules about confidentiality because if the Court permits it they will see the papers in the case. It will also be important for them to have no personal interest in the case.

COURT FORMS AND FEES

You will usually have to pay a fee to bring an application before the Court. Your local Court Office or the HMCTS website will be able to tell you how much you have to pay. The fee for making an application for a Child Arrangements Order is presently £215.00.

If, during a case that has already begun, you need to make an application for an urgent hearing, or to adjourn a hearing date, you may also have to pay a fee.

Exemption from fees

You can be exempt from paying fees if you receive certain state benefits (for example, income support) or if your income is below a set level. Again, your local Court Office or the HMCTS website should be able to give you the information to work out whether you have to pay. There is a fee exemption form EX160A for those eligible.

Forms

It is important that you use the correct form for the application you are making. The main forms and court fees at the time of writing this book are:

◆ An application for a Child Arrangements Order, £215 on Form C100 (and C1A if there are allegations of harm)

◆ An application for Parental Responsibility, £215 on Form C1 (and C1A if there are allegations of harm)

◆ An application for a Prohibited Steps or Specific Issue Order, £215 on Form C100 (and C1A if there are allegations of harm)

◆ An application to enforce a Child Arrangements Order, £215 on Form C79

◆ An application for Directions in a case already before the Court, £155 on Form C2 without consent or £50 if by consent

◆ An application for a Non-Molestation or Occupation Order No Fee, Form FL404 for an Occupation Order, FL404A for a Non-Molestation Order

Court forms can be obtained either from your local Family Court or are downloadable at www.justice.gov.uk/forms.

APPLYING FOR AN ORDER IN RESPECT OF A CHILD

The court process for applying for a Child Arrangements Order, Specific Issue or Prohibited Steps Order starts with the filing of a Form C100. This is the form filed by the Applicant and it sets out what Order is being sought and the reasons why. 'Filing' is when you take the form to the Court Office to be processed. The C100 is a very straightforward form.

If you consider that your home address is 'confidential', perhaps as a result of domestic violence in the relationship, then you can ask the Court for the address to be made confidential on all court papers. The Judge has the power to allow your address to remain confidential from other parties, although it is usual for the Court to have the address. You will still need a correspondence address.

If you need permission to apply for an Order, then you still use Form C100 but specify that you are asking for permission as part of your application.

It is essential that the Form C100 also makes it clear that mediation in this case is either not appropriate or has been tried but did not succeed. Otherwise the form may need to be signed by the mediator.

If you are alleging that the child is at risk of harm, then you need to also prepare Form C1A. It is important to raise such issues at the earliest opportunity.

You then take the completed forms to the Court Office for issuing. Once your application has been issued, it means it is 'live' and will only come to an end if the Court makes a Final Order, strikes out the application or gives you permission to withdraw it.

The appropriate respondents to the Application will be anyone who holds Parental Responsibility for the child. This will include the Local Authority (Social Services) if they have it under a Care Order.

Notice in Form C6 will also be given to anyone providing the child with accommodation, and anyone with whom the child has lived for three years.

At this stage, the first of the requirements of the Child Arrangements Programme will take effect and Police checks, discussions with CAFCASS and allocation to the appropriate level of the Family Court will take place.

In the ordinary way of things, the application will be served (usually by the Court) no later than 14 days before the first court hearing. The Court has the power in urgent cases to shorten this time.

Anyone responding to an application must file with the Court and serve on the parties an acknowledgement in Form C7 and again, a Form C1A if harm is alleged, within 14 days of being served with the Order.

The Court will set a hearing date and will give directions as to what should happen before then. Read it carefully and make sure you do what is required of you before the hearing to avoid any delay.

APPLYING FOR AN ADJOURNMENT

There may be times in court proceedings when you cannot attend court, due to unforeseen circumstances.

The important thing in these situations is that you tell the Court and the other side and apply for an adjournment in good time, if possible. Even if the other side agrees, the Court will still need to be notified. This can be done by way of a letter or by filing a proper application in a Form A. The Court Office will be able to help you as to which method to use. You are likely to require evidence such as a medical note, where appropriate, or a letter from your employers if you have to work.

If you do not attend court without good reason and without giving as much notice as you can and/or without an adjournment being granted by the Court, the case could carry on in your absence and important decisions be made that can concern you without your input.

5

Parental Responsibility

The Children Act makes it clear that the language to be used by parents must convey that they do not have formal rights with regard to their children, but that they can have Parental Responsibility, or, as it is often known, PR.

DEFINING PARENTAL RESPONSIBILITY

The legal definition of Parental Responsibility within the Children Act is 'all the rights, duties, powers, responsibilities and authority which by law a parent of a child has in relation to the child and his property'.

The Court considers that bringing up children is the responsibility of both parents and the principal role of the State is to help rather than interfere.

PR represents 'the fundamental status of parents'. This means that by having PR you hold a formal status in law.

Where two people have PR they share it equally. It should also be noted that more than one or two people can have PR for a child. If a child lives with a relative under a Child Arrangements Order, that relative will have PR alongside the two parents.

It should be noted that the fact that a person has or does not have Parental Responsibility for a child shall not affect any financial obligations which he may have to the child or any rights in relation to the child's death.

CONSULTING OTHERS WITH PARENTAL RESPONSIBILITY

Do I need to consult others with PR on every issue?
On a day-to-day basis, where more than one person has PR for a child, each of them may act alone and without the other in meeting this responsibility.

It is common sense that a parent can make normal decisions with regard to the child's care and needs without checking with the other. Equally the Court would not be interested in micromanaging a child's every waking moment and nor should the absent parent.

The Court expects both parents to act like adults and put the child's needs first. This can of course be very complicated, particularly where the parents have split up and there is a degree of animosity between them. However, the Court will expect the child, even under such circumstances, to be the priority and for the parents to work together for the welfare of the child.

So which decisions need consultation and agreement?
There is no hard and fast rule. The type of decisions where all parents with PR should be consulted and have an equal input into

the decision-making process are schooling, change of name, the child's religion, serious medical problems and other important occurrences.

It is also the case that many professionals, such as school teachers, the Police, doctors, hospitals, Social Services and other organisations will not be able to deal as fully with a parent unless they have Parental Responsibility.

This means that you cannot decide important things about your child without consulting the other person. The Court expects you to respect the role of the other parent for the benefit of the child and to put aside differences to ensure that the child has a relationship with both parents.

The mother with PR does not have any greater emphasis in the decision-making process regarding a child than a father with PR. In the eyes of the law there is equality. Decisions with regard to the child should be made jointly and after discussion between all those people with PR, even where the parents have split up and the child lives with only one of the parents.

If agreement on such issues cannot be reached then either parent can make an application to the Court to determine the issue. This will usually be for a Specific Issue Order (see page 6).

It is of course always better if at all possible to agree the issue between the parents. The Court considers it as a fundamental duty that those with Parental Responsibility should work together.

UNDERSTANDING WHO HAS PARENTAL RESPONSIBILITY

Do I have Parental Responsibility?
Many parents will have Parental Responsibility without actually being aware that they do. There is no specific certificate you get from the hospital confirming you have PR.

As the mother, whether you are married or not, you will automatically have Parental Responsibility because you gave birth to the child. As such you do not need to do anything else.

In law, fathers do not automatically have Parental Responsibility for their children and you will need to consider this more closely.

Can other people have Parental Responsibility?
Others, besides parents, can have PR for a child. This could include a Local Authority under a Care Order for a child in care, a child's guardian or their grandparents or other relatives under a Child Arrangements Order.

How does a father get Parental Responsibility?
A father gets PR if:

1. the mother and father were married to each other at the time of the child's birth, the father will have Parental Responsibility for the child;

2. the mother and father were not married to each other at the time of the child's birth, the father obtains Parental Responsibility;

   (a) by jointly registering the father's name on the child's birth certificate (for births registered after 1 December 2003); or

(b) by re-registering the birth for a pre-December 2003 registration to add the father's name to the birth certificate. This can only be done with the attendance of the mother or a formal declaration of her consent that the father's name is to be added to the birth certificate. This can also only be done if the father's name was omitted from the original birth certificate;

(c) by subsequently marrying the mother of the child, the father automatically will obtain PR;

(d) getting a Parental Responsibility Agreement with the child's mother on a Form C(PRA)1;

(e) an Order of the Court granting the father Parental Responsibility;

(f) an Order of the Court that the child lives with the father under a Child Arrangements Order;

(g) by obtaining an Adoption Order from the Court;

(h) a step-parent can obtain PR with the consent of all those who already hold PR for the child on a Form C(PRA)2

Can Parental Responsibility for a child be removed?
A mother can only lose PR with regard to one of her children if the Court orders that child to be adopted from her care.

A father can also lose PR when the Court orders the child to be adopted from his care. A mother cannot simply remove PR from a father because she wants to or she considers him troublesome. Where a father has acquired Parental Responsibility for the child by virtue of a Parental Responsibility Agreement, Court Order or having been registered on the child's birth certificate, he can lose Parental Responsibility by order of the Court. This is a very draconian Order and the Court will rarely make such an Order and only where there has been extreme behaviour by the father. A child can also make this application provided that he has the Court's permission and can show that he understands the application.

How long does Parental Responsibility last?

Parental Responsibility, unless discharged, runs until the child reaches the age of 18.

Step-Parents and Parental Responsibility

If a child's parent (who has PR for the child) marries or becomes the civil partner of a person who is not the child's parent, the step-parent can acquire Parental Responsibility for the child if:

The parent (together with the other parent of the child if they also have PR) agrees for the step-parent to be granted PR. This can be agreed on the Parental Responsibility Agreement Form C(PRA)2.

The step-parent makes an application for Parental Responsibility and the Court makes an Order granting it.

The step-parent has a Child Arrangements Order made in their favour.

If the biological father of the child does not have PR, then the mother can enter into a Parental Responsibility Agreement with any step-parent without obtaining the consent of the biological father. If, however, the biological father has PR then his consent would be required before entering into such an agreement for it to be valid.

The biological father will not lose his PR simply because a step-parent also now has PR.

An 'unmarried' step-father cannot acquire Parental Responsibility by way of a Parental Responsibility Agreement or Court Order, but can apply to the Court to adopt the child.

Same-Sex Parents
It should be noted that this area of law with respect to Parental Responsibility is extremely complicated with the law continuing to develop and it is always advisable to get legal advice before issuing court proceedings.

Conception on or after 6 April 2009
Lesbian couples who are civil partners at the time of conception and conceive a child through artificial insemination (it must be noted that the non-birth mother must consent to the conception) will both automatically be treated as their child's legal parents and as such can both be named on the birth certificate and have Parental Responsibility. Where a child has a mother and a second female parent, he or she does not have a legal father. If the non-birth mother is not registered as a 'parent' on the birth certificate then she can enter into a Parental Responsibility Agreement with the mother's consent by completing a Form C(PRA)3 or by making an application to the Court for a Child Arrangements Order or for Parental Responsibility.

Lesbian couples who are not civil partners at the time of conception, but who conceive together through a fertility clinic (as licensed in the UK by the Human Fertilisation and Embryology Authority), may also both be treated as legal parents. Both parties must sign the election forms, which are provided by the clinic before the date of conception. The non-birth mother can then be named on the birth certificate if her partner consents and for those children conceived on or after 6 April 2009 she will also have Parental Responsibility.

If the non-birth parent is not named on the birth certificate she can obtain Parental Responsibility on the basis that both partners consent and complete a Parental Responsibility Agreement. If agreement cannot be reached then an application will need to be made to the Court for Parental Responsibility in the same way as set out above.

Where non-civil partners conceive outside of a UK-licensed clinic the non-birth mother will have to adopt the child to obtain Parental Responsibility.

Conception prior to 6 April 2009

For lesbian couples that have conceived children together before 6 April 2009 the law is very different. A non-birth partner will not automatically be classed as a parent, even if the couple were civil partners. To obtain Parental Responsibility the non-birth parent would need to make an application to the Court for a Child Arrangements Order, adoption of the child or by the completion of a Parental Responsibility Agreement on a Form C(PRA)3.

ENTERING INTO A PARENTAL RESPONSIBILITY AGREEMENT

The starting point is that when the relationship between the mother and father is going well there is really no need to enter into a Parental Responsibility Agreement. If the unmarried father for whatever reason is not listed on the birth certificate it generally will not be of issue when both parents are together in the relationship and spending time with the child. The need for agreement generally arises when the relationship has either ended or is coming to an end and the relationship is becoming somewhat strained. For some couples this is not the best time to discuss whether the father has Parental Responsibility or not.

To reach an agreement on the father obtaining Parental Responsibility, the process is to complete a PR Agreement. It must be completed on a specified form for it to have legal effect. It cannot be put together in a letter, by text or through a conversation. The Parental Responsibility Agreement must be completed on the specified Form C(PRA)1 and then processed by the local Family Court. A separate form must be used for each child.

It is recommended that both parents seek legal advice before completing the form so that you both understand your legal rights and the significance of the form. The procedure for completing the form C(PRA1) is very straightforward:

- both biological parents must attend to get the forms signed and witnessed;

- the child must be resident in England and Wales;

- a Justice of the Peace, a Justices' Clerk, an assistant to a Justices' Clerk, or a court official who is authorised to administer oaths will witness the parties' signatures and he or she will then sign the certificate of the witness;

- a Solicitor cannot witness your signature, nor indeed can anyone else;

- the mother when making her declaration will have to bring a copy of the child's birth certificate to court;

- both parents will also need evidence of their identity showing a photograph and signature (for example a passport, driving licence or official pass). The birth certificate cannot be accepted as sufficient proof of identity.

When the agreement has been signed and witnessed the original needs to be copied twice and then the form needs to be sent to the Principal Registry of the Family Division, First Avenue, 42–49 High Holborn, London WC1V 6NP.

There is presently no fee. The Registry will keep the original and the copies will be stamped and returned to the addresses on the form.

HOW DO I MAKE AN APPLICATION FOR PARENTAL RESPONSIBILITY FOR MY CHILD?

Generally fathers who make applications for Parental Responsibility combine this with an application for contact or to spend time with the child. This is often cheaper, quicker and makes common sense.

The application is made using Form C100. This needs to be accompanied by Form C1A if there has been violence, a fear of violence or other harm. You will also have to pay the court fee, which at the time of writing is £215.00. You should check with the Court whether that fee remains correct.

Before you can start court proceedings you will usually have to meet with a mediator, who will give you information about mediation and other dispute resolution options.

WHAT FACTORS WILL THE COURT CONSIDER IN DECIDING TO GRANT THE FATHER PARENTAL RESPONSIBILITY?

The Court will consider the following factors in deciding whether to grant PR:

◈ that the father is the biological father of the child;

◈ the level of commitment that the father has shown to the child. This is often a simple evidential test of the father's involvement in the child's life and upbringing;

◈ the degree of attachment between the father and the child;

◈ the reason for the father's application to the Court;

◈ any other relevant factors.

An application by a father for PR is asking the Court to recognise his position as the child's father. The Court looks at the application on its own merits and will consider any application to spend time with or live with the child separately. The Court will also consider that the welfare of the child is paramount and consult the Welfare Checklist. It is helpful for you if applying for Parental Responsibility to go through the Welfare Checklist, line by line, and make references in your evidence (be this in your application or any witness statement) to the specific elements of the Checklist.

The Court will also consider:

◈ The child's welfare – this is the most important factor. It will usually be in the child's interests for their father to be granted Parental Responsibility. This is because it shows the child that their father wants to be involved in their life and in most cases the Court wishes to promote the relationship between the father and their child. It is important for the child to know both sides of their family so that the child can understand its identity, its ethnicity and origin. However, there will be some cases where it is not in the child's interests for their father to have Parental Responsibility, perhaps where the father is to be in prison for the duration of the child's upbringing.

- The degree of commitment shown by the father to the child – this includes the efforts the father has made to see his child, remain in contact with the child, receive updates about them (for example from their nursery or school) and whether they have provided for them financially.

- The degree of attachment between the father and child – this means the relationship and bond that the father and child enjoy. For example, the father might see the child every weekend and the child talk about how much they enjoy seeing their father. On the other hand, the father may never have met the child (through choice or because the mother has not allowed it) and they may have no bond or attachment to each other. Photographs and copies of cards or letters may evidence a degree of attachment.

- The reasons why the father is applying for Parental Responsibility. The father may be applying for Parental Responsibility because he wishes to be recognised in law as the child's father and to be involved in decisions about the child's upbringing. On the other hand, the father might have applied for Parental Responsibility because he dislikes the mother and wishes to make her life difficult. The Court will be more supportive of an application if the reasons relate to the former rather than the latter.

◆ Any other relevant factors – this could be, for example, the commitment and attachment which the father has with his other children that he could use to suggest that he wishes to enjoy a similar relationship with this child. The fact that one of the reasons for applying is hostility between the parents is not in itself a reason for the Court to refuse Parental Responsibility.

All of these factors will be considered and the Court will decide how much weight to place on each factor in reaching its decision. It is in fact quite unusual for a Court to refuse a father's application for Parental Responsibility if the test is met and there would need to be a reason why it was not in the child's best interests. For this reason it is often more sensible for the mother to agree to the application.

GRANDPARENTS AND OTHER RELATIVES

What rights do grandparents have to see their grandchildren?

This issue of the rights of grandparents and other relatives as to spending time with a child is somewhat complicated.

In an ideal scenario, when a child is born to a family the parents would be delighted to allow all of the child's relatives to spend time with the child. This is in most cases perfectly natural. However, where parents have split up or there have been issues in the past, things can and sometimes do become more difficult. Some parents blame relatives for taking sides or interfering or have safeguarding concerns about the child's relatives. As a result, some grandparents do not see their grandchildren.

So what can grandparents do?

The starting point is always to speak with the parent with whom the child lives and try to reach an agreement without the need for court proceedings. It is usually in the child's best interests to spend time with grandparents. This is part of the child's history, ethnicity and identity. Sometimes other relatives can attempt to facilitate a compromise or mediation can be used.

Such an approach is always going to be better than having the court decide on such matters as it gives both parties more control and is less unpleasant.

However, there will be circumstances where this is not always possible. In such circumstances the grandparent will need to make an application to the Court to spend time with a child or children or, in some cases, they may make an application for the child or children to live with them.

Such an application is made using Form C100.

Grandparents might apply within proceedings already started by one of the parents. This may be the case where a father or mother has applied for a Child Arrangements Order because they are not seeing their child and the grandparents who are also not seeing the child may apply within those proceedings. In these circumstances the Court would either consolidate the proceedings once the grandparents have issued their Form C100 application for a Child Arrangements Order or allow the two cases to be heard at the same time.

Can grandparents automatically see children?

It may surprise you but grandparents do not have an automatically recognised status in law just because they are related to the child. They have no basic legal right to see the child.

The reality of course may be that the grandparents have played an important role in the child's life – for example, through regular contact, babysitting, financial support or childcare arrangements, including the child temporarily residing with them.

Grandparents will normally require the 'leave' of the Court, which is the Court's permission to make a Section 8 application.

In what circumstances do grandparents not need the Court's permission to apply for a Section 8 Order?

There are circumstances when a grandparent does not need to get the permission of the Court to apply for a Section 8 Order.

These are circumstances where, for example:

◆ the child has lived with them for at least 3 years (this does not have to be a continuous 3-year period – it must not have started more than 5 years before the application, or ended more than 3 months before the application);

◆ if there is a Child Arrangements Order in force which provides for the child to live with the grandparent;

◆ if the grandparent is a Guardian or Special Guardian of the child or if the grandparent has permission from all those with Parental Responsibility for the child.

However, if none of these criteria is fulfilled, the grandparents will require the permission of the Court to make a Section 8 application.

How does the Court decide whether to grant grandparents permission to make a Section 8 application?

Any person who is not automatically entitled to apply to the Court for a Child Arrangements Order may only make an application to the Court if they obtain the leave of the Court to do so.

It is important to note that the granting of leave does not raise any presumption that the grandparents' application for a Child Arrangements Order will be granted. It is simply the first step in the application process.

The grandparent must show that there are reasons why the Court should grant them permission to make this application.

In determining the application for permission, the principle that the child's welfare is paramount does not apply, nor does the Welfare Checklist strictly apply (although the factors may be relevant).

Instead the Court will primarily consider the following factors:

- the nature of the proposed application. In other words, the Court will consider what Order the grandparent is asking for;

- the applicant's connection with the child. The Court will consider what the relationship is between the child and the grandparent (including whether they are biologically related, how much time they have spent together, whether the grandparent has remained in contact with the child or attempted to remain in contact with the child, what the child's views are about their grandparents (if they are of sufficient age and understanding to explain this));

◆ any risk there might be of the proposed application disrupting the child's life to such an extent that he or she would be harmed by it. Harm means ill treatment or the impairment of health or development including, for example, impairment suffered from seeing or hearing the ill treatment of another. This includes the harm to the child of the application succeeding as well as the harm to the child of the application being made. For example, if a grandparent had been found to have abused a child and caused them harm, the child may suffer further harm from the grandparent making an application to have contact with them, as well as that application being granted;

◆ the merits of the proposed application, i.e. its prospects of success;

◆ if a Local Authority is looking after the child, the Court will also consider the Authority's plans for the child's future and the wishes and feelings of the child's parents.

The Court can also consider any other factors that are relevant to the question of whether a grandparent should be granted permission. The government appears to believe that this 'leave application' acts as an 'early filter' to determine which applications are in the best interests of the child and does not make it unduly difficult, particularly for grandparents, to be able to spend time with their grandchildren.

How does the Court view applications by relatives for Section 8 Orders?

The principle for other relatives, such as aunts and uncles, is the same as it is for grandparents and the same rules apply. Each application will be decided on the merits of the case. There may be some cases where the relative has played an extremely important part in the child's life and there are safeguarding concerns about the child continuing to reside with its parent. On the other hand, there may be some cases where the relative has no connection with the child and the Court considers that it is not in the child's interests for the relationship to be fostered – for example, where the relative is very bad at keeping in touch and is likely to let the child down. Other relatives, like grandparents, will need to apply for the leave of the Court prior to making an application, unless:

◆ the child has lived with them for at least 3 years (this does not have to be a continuous 3-year period – it must not have started more than 5 years before the application, or ended more than 3 months before the application);

◆ if there is a Child Arrangements Order in force which provides for the child to live with the relative;

◆ if the relative is a Guardian or Special Guardian of the child or if the relative has permission from all those with Parental Responsibility for the child.

However, if none of these criteria is fulfilled, the relative will require the permission of the Court to make a Section 8 application.

The next step

If the Court does grant a grandparent or relative permission to apply for a Section 8 Order this does not create a presumption that they will be successful in their application. The case will proceed in the normal way towards a Final Hearing. This means that the Court will consider what evidence is required, including whether to obtain a CAFCASS Section 7 Report and the exchange of any witness statements before listing the matter for a Final Hearing.

CAN OTHER PEOPLE MAKE AN APPLICATION FOR A SECTION 8 ORDER?

Other people may also need to seek the Court's permission before making an application for a Section 8 Order. They will need to do so unless they can satisfy the criteria for automatic permission (as set out above in relation to grandparents and relatives) or alternatively:

◆ they are a party to a marriage or a civil partner to a civil partnership (whether or not subsisting) in relation to whom the child is a child of the family, i.e. they are a step-parent to the child;

◆ they have Parental Responsibility for the child;

◆ the child has lived with them for at least one year prior to the making of an application relating to with whom the child should live and when the child is to live with any person.

If any other person does not have automatic permission, they too will need to satisfy the Court that they should be granted permission, having regard to the factors set out above in relation to grandparents.

Can a child make an application for a Section 8 Order?

A child can make an application for permission to apply for a Section 8 Order and, if successful, can become a party to private law proceedings between parents. The Court will consider whether the child has sufficient understanding to make the proposed application for the Section 8 Order. A CAFCASS officer may be asked to assist the Court in deciding this. Even if the child does have sufficient understanding, the Court is not bound to grant their application.

How does a person make an application for permission to apply for a Section 8 Order?

An application for permission must be made to the Court under Form C100. If there are ongoing proceedings in respect of the child, the application for permission must be served on all the parties in the case. If the application is freestanding, the Respondents to the application are the same as they would be if the application for permission is granted, i.e. those persons with Parental Responsibility for the child and/or any person with whom the child lives. An Application Notice must be prepared and must be served on each respondent.

The Application Notice must include:

◆ what Order is being sought; and

◆ why the applicant is seeking the Order.

The Application Notice must also include a draft of the Order being sought.

It should also be verified by a Statement of Truth if the applicant wishes to rely on the matters set out within the application as evidence.

Any written evidence in support should accompany the application. If you are the applicant, you will want to complete a witness statement setting out the grounds upon which the application is made – in other words, the reasons why you are asking the Court to grant you permission to apply for an Order. You should address each factor in turn.

If the parties agree on the terms of the Order sought, the Court can make the Order without the need for a hearing. If the parties do not agree on the terms of the Order sought, the Court will list the matter for a hearing unless it does not consider a hearing appropriate or the application is totally without merit.

Once the application for permission has been issued, the Court will list a hearing date and at this hearing will consider how best to hear the application. The Respondents to the application may not agree that you should be granted permission. The Court is likely to grant them time to respond to your statement with a statement of their own. This should address each of the grounds for permission and respond to the claims made by the applicant. For example, a grandparent may state that the child stayed with them each weekend and, as such, they have a close relationship. The respondent may state that the grandparent has only seen the child two or three times in the last year and that there is no relationship between them. If this is the case, the Court is likely to have to proceed to hear evidence on the issues between the parties. Alternatively the Court could order the parties to make submissions on the application and decide whether to grant permission without hearing any oral evidence.

If the permission is granted, the Court will then give direction to deal with the actual application. Just because leave to make the application is granted, it does not mean that the application itself will succeed.

If the application is dismissed, the grandparent or relative will no longer be part of any ongoing proceedings or, if the application was freestanding, the proceedings will come to an end. The grandparent or relative will have 21 days to appeal the decision not to grant them leave.

6

Holidays

GOING ABROAD

Where a parent has a Child Arrangements Order, which confirms that the child lives with them, they are able to take the child abroad for up to 28 days without the consent of any other person with Parental Responsibility. It is however common sense to discuss the holiday prior to booking it with anyone with Parental Responsibility and give them as much notice as possible.

You should discuss with them the nature, length and purpose of the holiday.

Notice is particularly important when the child will not be able to spend time with the absent parent as a result of the holiday. Arrangements should be agreed to allow for this parent to have some additional time either before or after the holiday. Consideration should also be given to whether some form of indirect contact (by telephone, Skype or FaceTime) could be facilitated during the holiday. This would be considered to be in the best interests of the child. If there is a Court Order in place that governs contact arrangements during a holiday, this will remain in place unless an application is made to vary or discharge it.

TAKING LONGER HOLIDAYS

For holidays of longer than 28 days, the written consent of every person with Parental Responsibility is required. If a child under the age of 16 years is removed or sent away for more than 28 days then this is an offence under the Child Abduction Act 1984, with the maximum penalty being up to seven years' imprisonment.

If a person with Parental Responsibility seeks to prevent another parent from taking the child on holiday where there is no Child Arrangements Order in place, then they will need to make an application to the Court for a Prohibited Steps Order. This would be made using the Form C100 (see page 211).

Equally, if the child lives with you and you do not have a Child Arrangements Order and the other person with Parental Responsibility refuses to consent to you taking the child on holiday abroad then you would need to apply to the Court for a Specific Issue Order. This application would be made using the Form C100.

What if I have a Special Guardianship Order?

If you have a Special Guardianship Order you may remove the child for up to three months without having to obtain the consents of other people with Parental Responsibility. For any periods over three months then you will require the consents of those with Parental Responsibility.

What will the Court consider when deciding whether a child should or should not be permitted to leave the country?

With either an application for a Prohibited Steps Order or a Specific Issue Order the Court will give consideration to the Welfare

Checklist and the principle that the child's welfare is the paramount consideration.

The Court is usually unlikely to prevent a child from going on a holiday unless the objecting parent can provide evidence that the holiday is not beneficial or that there is a degree of risk. It will not usually be enough to oppose a holiday because you cannot afford to take them abroad on holiday and you consider it unfair, or that you consider that they are treating their child differently to their step-children.

A holiday may not be considered beneficial when the child would be absent from school for a period of time or from examinations, miss important hospital or medical appointments; or indeed where the absent parent was suffering from significant ill health. The Court may also be reluctant to agree to a holiday where there is a lack of information as to the holiday destination, time frame or detail about the arrangements.

However, if it is just a holiday which is clearly beneficial to the child with no adverse consequences (other than the other party perhaps being unreasonable) it is very likely that the Court will allow the holiday.

If the proposed holiday was to a country or place that the Foreign Office was recommending that people do not visit, the Court would, however, have concerns. The Foreign Office has a website https://www.gov.uk/foreign-travel-advice that sets out the details of such countries/places and the reason why visits are not recommended.

Abduction of children

Another reason to object to a proposed holiday is the fear of child abduction. This is where you believe that the child may be permanently abducted to a foreign country (often referred to as jurisdiction) with the intention of them not being returned. If the proposed holiday is to a country which is not covered by the Hague Convention (see below) this will cause particular concern. The Hague Convention puts contracting states (countries) under an obligation to establish procedures to secure the prompt return of children 'wrongfully removed or retained in any contracting state' and to ensure that rights of custody are respected. States must use 'the most expeditious procedures available' to achieve these objectives. However, not all countries are members of the Hague Convention (and even when they are it is often not straightforward to recover a child). If the proposed holiday is to a country which is not a party to the Hague Convention then this may well be a reason to oppose the holiday and/or seek assurances for the child's return.

I want to go on holiday

When it comes to drafting your witness statement for the contested Final Hearing (see Chapter 14) the Court will require information about the proposed holiday. The Court will want to be reassured that you have properly considered the proposed arrangements and their impact on the child, including speaking to the child's school if the proposed holiday is during term time. It will assist your case if you can provide adequate detail and show that you have properly thought things out. The other parent may be alleging that you will not return to the UK. One of the purposes of your witness statement in such circumstances is to reassure the Court that this is not your intention and that you have clear plans to return and resume your life in the UK.

Therefore you may wish to consider the following factors when drafting your witness statement:

◆ reason for and purpose of the holiday;

◆ if the holiday is during school time, what does the school say about it? (You could obtain and exhibit written evidence from the school setting out whether the child will miss anything important, whether additional work can be given by the school to assist the child in catching up, etc.);

◆ detailed information as to the location of the holiday, the proposed accommodation and its address;

◆ detailed information about who else is going – this may include other relatives, siblings, a new partner, etc.;

◆ the child's wishes and feelings about the holiday;

◆ details of conversations you have had about the holiday with other persons who hold Parental Responsibility for the child;

◆ any connection which you, your family or the child has to the destination;

◆ any previous visits to this destination;

◆ the ties which you have to the UK;

◆ details of your employment and assets (e.g. property, business) in the UK.

I object to the holiday

If you object to the holiday then you would need to make an urgent application to the Court for a Prohibited Steps Order (see page 211).

You will need to have a genuine objection to the holiday and you will also need to show the Court that you are being reasonable and child focused. A genuine objection might be that the child misses an important examination. An unreasonable objection might be that the child will not be able to see you over a weekend when you usually spend time together. You may be of the view that the other parent intends to abduct the child and fail to return to the UK. You will need to prepare a witness statement for the Final Hearing (see Chapter 14) that explains why you object to the proposed holiday and why, if applicable, you believe that the other parent intends to abduct the child. You may wish to consider the following factors:

◆ why you oppose the holiday;

◆ details of conversations you have had with the parent proposing to take the child on holiday;

◆ the other parent's connection to the country that they propose to visit;

◆ whether the other parent has family or property in the country that they are proposing to visit;

◆ whether or not the country is governed by the Hague Convention;

◆ the other parent's connection to the UK (e.g. whether they have employment or any assets in the UK; whether they have any family who reside in the UK);

◆ the length of the holiday;

◆ whether the child will miss school or any examinations;

◆ the consequence of missing school (you may wish to obtain written evidence from the school setting out the impact on the child of missing the proposed time at school);

◆ any other relevant information.

Putting practical safeguards in place

The Court can put safeguards in place to allow the holiday to take place while attempting to ensure that the child will return at the end of the holiday. While this is not an exhaustive list, it could include all or any of the following:

◆ advice from an expert in the country that the child is visiting;

◆ formally confirming that the child is habitually resident in the UK;

◆ mirror Court Orders (e.g. an order permitting the child to be taken to a place on holiday for a certain period of time but also being made in the country where the holiday is to be taken);

◆ monetary bond (i.e. the parent who is taking the child on holiday depositing money with the Court);

◆ make the child a Ward of Court during the child's minority. This means that no important step can be taken in the child's life without the Court's permission and is an Order from the High Court, which carries weight in other countries;

◆ copies of all travel documents to provide the Court and the parties with the exact details of the travel arrangements;

◆ a transcript of the judgment (i.e. a word-for-word record of the Court's judgment) to be placed on the court file and permission given to disclose it to a foreign court, a foreign lawyer, qualified translator or expert witness employed or retained in the case.

What should I do if I fear abduction?

The first thing you should do if you fear the imminent abduction of your child from the UK (i.e. within a few hours) is to contact the Police. They may be able to issue an All Ports Alert to try to prevent a child from leaving the UK.

If you have the child's passport you should ensure that you keep it in a safe and secure place.

Prior to any removal of your child from the UK, you can also apply to the Family Court for one of the following remedies:

- **a Child Arrangements Order**, which settles with whom the child lives. The making of a Child Arrangements Order automatically provides that no person may remove the child to whom the Order relates from the UK for a period of longer than 28 days without either the written consent of each person who has Parental Responsibility for him or the permission of the Court;

- **Wardship Proceedings** for an Order making a child a Ward of Court. The result is that no important step in child's life may be taken without the permission of the Court;

- an Injunction under the Inherent Jurisdiction of the High Court, which prohibits the child's removal from the jurisdiction;

- **a Prohibited Steps Order** (see page 211);

- **a Specific Issue Order** (see page 212).

If a child has been abducted and removed from the UK and a criminal offence has been committed, extradition proceedings may be commenced where an extradition treaty exists with the country to which the abductor has gone. Extradition can only require the return of the alleged offender, not of the child. However, in many cases the child may also, for practical reasons, return with the alleged offender.

There are two specific international conventions relating to child abduction which have force in UK law. These are the Hague Convention and the European Convention. The details concerning these Conventions are outside the scope of this book. If you are concerned about your child being abducted then you should immediately contact a family lawyer for specialised assistance.

APPLYING TO PERMANENTLY REMOVE YOUR CHILD FROM THE JURISDICTION

Generally people seek to move abroad because they are going home, following a job or a new partner or are simply looking for a fresh start. Whatever the reason, when they are looking to take their children with them, then this will usually cause a significant change for those people in the child's life who are being left behind.

If you wish to live abroad with your child permanently, you need to obtain the written consent of all those people who have Parental Responsibility.

If they refuse to give their consent then you will have to make an application to the Court. This is often referred to as an application to remove the child from the jurisdiction permanently. This is a very difficult area of law and as such it is often beneficial to take legal advice as to the specifics of your case before issuing court proceedings.

The law

The leading case law on this area are: Re F (Relocation) [2013] 1
FLR 645, K v K (Relocation: Shared Care Arrangement) [2012] 2
FLR 880 and Payne v Payne [2001] 1 FLR 1052 which confirms that
the child's welfare is the paramount consideration and the Welfare
Checklist is the Court's starting point when considering these
applications.

The Court also recognises that if it allows a child to live
permanently in a foreign country, this would be a significant
interference with the Article 8 rights (right to respect for family
life) of the other parent and of any child. This can only be justified
by pressing concerns for the child's welfare and must be considered
reasonable, proportionate and in accordance with the law. There is
no presumption in favour of the parent applying to remove the child
from the jurisdiction.

Applications to relocate the child are more likely to be granted to a
parent who is the child's primary carer and/or when there is a Child
Arrangements Order in favour of that parent. In situations where
there is a genuine 'shared care' parenting arrangement in place, the
situation is more complicated and permission is less likely to be
granted to a parent seeking to relocate the child abroad.

The Court will consider the impact on the child's welfare if it
grants or refuses permission to relocate permanently. It will also
consider the impact on the child's parents, particularly in relation
to their ongoing relationship with their children. The Court will
also want to ensure that the move is genuine, well thought out and
considered.

DRAFTING THE WITNESS STATEMENT – POINTS TO CONSIDER

When it comes to drafting your witness statement for the contested Final Hearing, the Court will require information on the following:

- detailed reason for the move;

- links to the country which you are moving to (e.g. you may have already secured a job or you may have family members who already reside there and are willing to support you until you have a job);

- any immigration or visa issues;

- detailed information as to the location of the move and the accommodation in which you intend to reside;

- detailed information about any new partner (if appropriate) and any other persons with whom the child will live;

- the child's wishes and feelings about the proposed move;

- detailed information as to the nursery/school/facilities where the child will attend (it will assist if you can show that you have taken the time to speak to the proposed school and have confirmation that a place for the child is available upon your arrival). You may wish to obtain written evidence from the school that confirms that a place is available and that confirms the subjects/facilities available to the child. This is preferable to a school prospectus/brochure, although that can also be exhibited to your statement);

- details of any particular opportunities for the child (for example, the child may be particularly good at a sport and the proposed school may have excellent facilities for that sport);

◆ if you are proposing to work, details of the position, salary and length of contract;

◆ what support network is in place for you and the child;

◆ healthcare and medical facilities (this will be particularly important if the child has any health condition that requires regular medical intervention);

◆ any special considerations, such as culture, welfare, religion or ethnicity;

◆ details of the consequences of not being permitted to move;

◆ details of your proposals for the child to maintain contact with the other parent and any other relatives (this may include arrangements for school holidays, cost of air travel and accommodation, Skype, FaceTime, telephone, etc.). It is extremely important that you can show the Court that you have thought about how the child can continue a relationship with the other parent and that you have proposals, which can mitigate, to some extent, the impact that moving to another country will have on this. The Court will consider it to be in the child's best interests to continue a relationship with their other parent and other relatives and it will assist your case if you can show that you accept this and have clear and child-focused proposals;

◆ details of any conversations that you have had with the other parent.

OBJECTING TO YOUR CHILD BEING REMOVED FROM THE JURISDICTION

If you object to the removal of the child from the jurisdiction and the parent who proposes to relocate with the child has not made an application to court, you should make an urgent application to the Court for a Prohibited Steps Order (see page 211). You will need to prepare a witness statement, which sets out in a clear and concise manner the reasons for your objection to the proposed relocation. You may wish to address the following factors in your witness statement:

- the reasons why you oppose the proposed move;

- how the time that you spend with the child will change as a result of the move;

- which other family members or friends will suffer a change of relationship as a result of the move (grandparents, aunts, uncles, other siblings, etc. You may also wish to obtain statements from these relatives to support your case);

- how the child's schooling will be affected in comparison to the present arrangement;

- any healthcare or medical changes arising from the move compared with the present arrangements;

- you should also set out in detail (and where possible with evidence) any concerns or questions that you have with the other parent's relocation plans;

- details of conversations which you have had with the parent who is proposing to relocate the child;

- any language or cultural difficulties that there are likely to be;

- any financial issues that you consider relevant;

- the child's wishes and feelings;

- details of how you would feel if the proposed move took place.

APPLYING FOR PASSPORTS

Children need to have their own valid passports to travel abroad. Any person with Parental Responsibility can apply for a child's passport. However, they must notify everyone else with Parental Responsibility who may raise an objection. If one person with Parental Responsibility has already applied for a passport for the child and the application has been issued, you will not be able to apply for another passport for the child, even if you have Parental Responsibility for that child. There is no ownership of a passport – in other words, just because it has been paid for by one parent does not mean that they have sole use or right to it.

Objecting to the issuing of a passport

If you object to the issuing of a child's passport to another person with Parental Responsibility, you should write to the regional office of the HM Passport Office and request that they do not issue a passport to a child. Such an objection can be lodged if the Court has issued one of the following Orders:

◆ Prohibited Steps Order;

◆ Child Arrangements Order (if the objector is the person in whose favour the CAO has been made);

◆ an Order confirming that the Court has not approved a removal of the child from the jurisdiction or that the objector's consent to such a removal is necessary;

◆ an Order, which requires the surrender of a UK passport and prohibiting a further application being made for a passport.

If there are no Orders as set out above, an objection can still be considered if brought by the mother or the Police where no other person has Parental Responsibility and they are raising a concern under the Child Abduction Act 1984. In addition, if you are in the process of applying for any of the above Orders you should notify the HM Passport Office of this and provide them with the date of any court hearing where you expect the Court to make a relevant Order. You should then update them accordingly after the court hearing and the making of any Order.

It is important to note that the HM Passport Office cannot prevent a person obtaining a passport for a child from another country's Embassy, High Commission or Consulate in this country. If the other parent is not a British national or has dual nationality, it is sensible to write a letter to the Embassy or Consulate of their country asking them not to issue a passport to your child. They are not obliged to comply with your request but may do so voluntarily. There is also merit in writing to your MP and alerting them to the issue.

7

Moving Within the UK

If a parent intends to move locally with the child this is not
something that requires the consent of other people with Parental
Responsibility prior to the move. The Court will not usually be
concerned with a local move. However, the exception may be
where the proposed move results in a change of school for the
child and this is not agreed between those persons with Parental
Responsibility.

However, moves of a greater distance are becoming more common.
If a parent decides to move with a child from Birmingham to
St Ives, for example, the Court may have to become involved
if the other parent objects to the proposed move. An important
consideration will be whether the existing arrangements for the
child to see their other parent can carry on. If you want to move
house and this will mean that you can no longer comply with a
Court Order, it is your responsibility to apply to vary the Order
on notice to the other side and in plenty of time.

The starting point always is to discuss the potential move with
the other parent (or people with Parental Responsibility) and see
whether an agreement can be reached (unless this puts you or the

child in danger). The basis of agreement may be that the 'absent' parent gets to spend greater time with the child at weekends or during school holidays. It could also include an agreement that handovers take place at a venue halfway between the two homes or that one party undertakes one journey and the other parent undertakes the return journey. These are practical solutions to a difficult arrangement.

The law does not prevent parents from moving from one part of the country to another. However, there is guidance for the Court when dealing with applications from parents seeking to move with a child or parents seeking to prevent the child moving away.

If agreement cannot be reached, the person seeking to move with the child needs to make an application to the Court for a Specific Issue Order (see on page 212) while the person opposing the move would need to apply to the Court for a Prohibited Steps Order (see page 211). This is a difficult area of the law and it is always beneficial to take urgent legal advice before issuing proceedings.

THE LAW

The leading cases on this area are Payne v Payne [2001] EWCA Civ 166, K v K (Relocation: Shared Care Arrangement) [2011] EWCA Civ 793; [2012] 2 FLR 880, Re F (Relocation) [2012] EWCA Civ 1364; [2013] 1 FLR 645 and Re TC and JC (Children: Relocation) [2013] 2 FLR 484. There has also developed a principle called the 'exceptionality test', that is often cited as an authority, which allows a parent to relocate a child within the UK unless there are exceptional circumstances to prohibit it. The difficulty with the law is that there is no definition of what exceptional means and as such the Court will decide this on a case-by-case basis.

While case law is never straightforward, the general principle to be applied by the Courts when considering whether or not to allow internal relocation is that the welfare of the child (the Welfare Checklist) is paramount and overrides all other considerations, however powerful they may be. This means that the Court will consider the elements of the Welfare Checklist when deciding whether or not to permit the relocation. A Child Arrangements Order naming both parents as being with whom the child lives in a shared care arrangement does not necessarily prevent an internal relocation.

DRAFTING YOUR WITNESS STATEMENT

When it comes to drafting your witness statement for the contested Final Hearing (see page 147) the Court will require information on the following:

◆ detailed reason for the move;

◆ details of the conversations you have had with the other parent to try to reach agreement;

◆ links to the area which you are proposing to move to (e.g. employment, family, new partner);

◆ detailed information as to the location and proposed accommodation;

◆ detailed information about any new partner (if appropriate) or any person with whom the child will live;

◆ the child's wishes and feelings about the proposed move;

◆ detailed information as to the nursery/school/facilities where the child will attend (it is a good idea to exhibit something in writing from the proposed school which confirms that the child has a place at the school and the subjects/facilities they are able to offer the child. A school brochure/prospectus/Ofsted Report is also useful but the Court will not be impressed if you have not spoken to the school to confirm arrangements);

- if you are proposing to work, details of the position, salary and length of contract;

- what support network is in place for you and the child in the new area;

- details of the consequences of not being permitted to move;

- what proposals you have for the child to maintain contact with the other parent. This may include arrangements for school holidays, Skype, FaceTime, telephone, etc. As set out above in relation to relocating abroad, it is very important to show the Court that you recognise the importance of the child maintaining their relationship with their family and that you have thought out how this can practically work.

WHAT IF I OBJECT TO MY CHILD MOVING?

If you object to the child moving and the other parent has not made an application to court then you would need to make an urgent application to the Court for a Prohibited Steps Order (see page 211). In your witness statement you should consider the following matters:

- why you oppose the move;

- how the time that you spend with the child will change as a result of the move;

◆ which other family members or friends will suffer a change of relationship as a result of the move (grandparents, aunts, uncles, other siblings, etc. You may also wish to obtain statements from these relatives to support your case);

◆ details of the conversations you have had with the parent who proposes to move;

◆ how the child's schooling will be affected in comparison to the present arrangement. You may be able to refer to OFSTED documents as comparisons;

◆ any healthcare or medical changes arising from the move compared with the present arrangements;

◆ you should also set out in detail (and where possible with evidence) any concerns or questions that you have with the other parent's relocation plans;

◆ any relevant financial issues;

◆ the child's wishes and feelings;

◆ details of how you would feel if the proposed move took place.

ABDUCTION AND RELOCATION WITHIN ENGLAND AND WALES

Where a parent takes the child from the care of the other parent and refuses to return them, it is possible to get an Order from the Court to require the parent or government agency, or anyone who may have information about where the child is, to disclose what they know. This information can then be used to help get your child back.

If the parent who has taken the child does not have Parental Responsibility for that child it may be easier for the Police to assist in returning the child without involving the Court.

If the Police say they cannot assist you without a Court Order, then you need to go to court to get one. Situations like this are almost always urgent and the Court will have procedures in place so that your case can be heard quickly.

You do not need to use a different set of court forms just because a case is urgent. Just fill in the correct court form for the application you want to make, whether that is a Child Arrangements Order that your child should be returned to your care or an Order asking for the Police to be authorised to help, and make sure you make it clear on the form that your case is urgent.

If you explain this at the Court office, they can make arrangements for you to see the Judge early. If you feel that you can give some notice to the other parent of what you are doing, then you should try. If you think that letting them know will make it harder to get your child back (if, for example, you are worried that they will leave the area) then you need to make your application without this notice. Again, you will need to explain why you are doing this on the form. The Judge will then see you and decide what steps need to be taken.

WHAT DO I DO IF MY CHILD IS TAKEN?

Where there is already a Court Order in place
Whether there are any Court Orders in place will be relevant. If you have an Order that the child is to live with you and the other parent has kept the child outside of their contact times, then this will be a breach of that Order.

The Court has powers to make urgent Orders in these circumstances. Which Order you apply for will depend on the legal situation of your particular case.

Where no Court Order is in place

If there are no Court Orders in force, you may need to ask for an Order that the child lives with you and a direction that the child is delivered to your care. This will be done using a Child Arrangements Order for the child to live with you and a Specific Issue Order to require the child to be returned. You should apply to the Court immediately and ask the Court to deal with the matter urgently.

The Court can be asked to deal with the matter on an 'ex parte' or without notice basis. This basically means you are making an application to court without the other person knowing.

An Order for a child to live with a parent made without the other party knowing about it is a very unusual Order for the Court to make and requires a high level of evidence. Good reasons for applying without notice can be if you are genuinely afraid as to the actions the parent may take if he or she became aware of your application.

RECOVERY ORDER

Where an Order for a child to live with a parent is in force and the child is being kept away in breach of that Order, you can ask for an Order authorising a Police Officer to recover the child, although it is important to remember that this Order is intended to give them permission to act. It does not require them to do anything.

The application for an Order to authorise the Police to act is made under Section 34 of the Children Act 1989. You apply for this Order on Form C3 and your application should be supported by a witness statement (see page 164). Technically you should also provide the Court with a 'draft order', although the Judge may help with this while at court. A draft order is basically the Order that you would like the Judge to make.

It is also a good idea to allow the other side a short period to return the child before the Police go to collect the child because that could be unpleasant for the child to witness.

It is an application that can be made with or without notice to the other party. If you feel that making the application and giving notice to the other side will cause the child to be moved to another location, you may want to consider applying without notice. If this is not a risk, then the Court may expect you to give some notice to the other side.

As with any application you make without telling the other side, you will need to make sure you explain in your evidence why you did not give notice and it remains open to the Court to adjourn your application until notice is given.

Where you are required to serve the other side and give them notice, one day's notice is usually appropriate as it is an emergency situation, and it is preferable that you arrange for the other side to be served personally as this will ensure that the Court will be satisfied the other side is aware of the hearing. Personal service is where the papers are given personally to the other side usually by a process server (usually you can find a local process server on the Internet), not just posted to their address.

WHAT IF I DO NOT KNOW WHERE MY CHILD IS?

If your child has been taken and you do not know where the child is, you can ask the Court for an Order against named people who may know where they are. These applications are treated by the Courts as emergency applications and, again, they can be made without notice. They are made on Form C4 and a copy of the draft order, which you also need to provide to the Court, is on Form C30. The procedure is the same as for a Recovery Order (see above).

The effect of the Order is to require 'any person' to provide the Court any information they may have as to the whereabouts of a child.

However, where the child is living within a refuge the address of the refuge should not be disclosed to anyone other than the Court Manager, for the protection of the other families who may be present there. Even lawyer–client privilege cannot be used to withhold information as to the location of a child and so you may be able to get Orders against the other parent's Solicitor, or former Solicitor.

If an Order is made, but the person named in it does not comply, the Court can, provided the Order was properly served with the correct Notice on it, punish the person in breach as a contempt of court. This can include imprisonment.

IF YOU FIND YOURSELF CONSIDERING NOT RETURNING YOUR CHILD IN BREACH OF A COURT ORDER

If you are thinking about not returning your child when a Court Order requires you to, this a serious step and you must think very carefully. You need to consider why you are not willing to return the child and look at all of your options. If a young child is simply saying they do not want to go home, and there is no clear reason then keeping the child and not returning them is harder to justify.

If, however, you have immediate concerns about the safety of your child when with his or her other parent, then that may be another matter. Even then, you will need to make sure you take all proper steps and look at the evidence of harm. If your child has bruises and is making allegations that this was done deliberately by the other parent, then this is a serious situation and you will need some advice from child protection professionals.

You should make Children Services or the Police aware of your concerns if they are significant and seek their advice.

You will need advice as to what circumstances make it appropriate not to return a child. If you act in line with the advice you received, this will help protect you if you are criticised later.

You should usually raise your concerns with the other parent to see if there is a reasonable explanation. If there is not, or the concerns prevail, then you should make an urgent application to the Court for a Child Arrangements Order. Again, this application will be made in the same way as a normal application. You still use the same forms (C100/C1A) but explain on the form that it is urgent and ask for an urgent hearing. You need to consider whether you should give notice to the other side. Where possible, notice should be given unless that would cause a risk to the child.

As is clear from this chapter, there are a number of Orders that can be made to secure the return of children and to avoid these steps being taken. It is advisable for you to apply to the Court as early as possible for an Order to protect your position until your concerns can be investigated. You will need to consider whether you need to give Notice of your application to the other side.

It is very rare for the Court to make Orders changing where a child lives without notice to the other side. If Orders are made, they are usually made for a short period of time, often just until a full hearing can take place.

At hearings that take place without notice, the Judge will just see you in his courtroom. As the other side will not be there to argue their side, the Court will want to be as balanced as possible. The Judge will pay the most attention to the written information you have provided because copies of that can be given to the other side after the hearing, whereas things you say in court cannot. Therefore it is most important that your paperwork says everything you want it to.

The Judge will set a date for the case to come back with the other side also there.

8

Schooling and Other Issues

CHANGING SCHOOL

Education is an important part of a child's upbringing. The Court would expect parents to work together to determine important questions around a child's schooling. Just because a child does not reside with a particular parent does not prevent that parent from having a contribution to make in choosing a school. This can be the case whether a parent has Parental Responsibility or not.

Parents ideally should discuss school choices well in advance of any planned change of school. Many schools will be able to arrange separate dates for parents to have a look around the premises and speak to staff.

If parents cannot agree over a choice of school, or whether a child should be educated at home, the Court exists as a last resort. The main ways in which the Court can be asked to deal with the question of schooling are either:

◆ an application for a Specific Issue Order to allow a child to attend a particular school;

◆ an application for a Prohibited Steps Order to prevent a child from changing schools.

Both applications are to be made under Section 8 of the Children Act 1989. Unless applications are urgent then you will be expected to go through the process of mediation first.

Circumstances such as a parent becoming aware that the other parent imminently intends to change the child's school without consultation, especially where the change is one that is not in the child's best interests, may justify an urgent application. An urgent application starts with exactly the same paperwork as a standard application. In the case of a Prohibited Steps Order or a Specific Issue Order, that is Form C100/C1A. You will need to make it clear on the form that it is an urgent application and that a hearing date is needed quickly. You also need to explain this to the court staff.

You will be expected to give some notice to the other side, unless to do so places the child at risk.

A parent without Parental Responsibility cannot change a child's school without an Order.

What will the Court consider?
In order to decide which school a child should attend, or whether they should change schools, the Court will need as much information about the choice of school as possible. OFSTED reports are a useful source of information about a school's strengths and weaknesses. The school's website or brochure is also a good source of information. It is unlikely that the Court would hear oral evidence from staff at the school.

The Court is also likely to be helped by information about the child themselves and particularly if they have any educational needs. Your child's school reports could again be useful evidence, together with any statement of special educational needs or EHC (Education, Health and Care) plans.

If, for example, your child shows a particular aptitude in a subject and the school you wish them to attend is particularly good in that subject, this can be an important part of your argument.

If the change of school comes as part of your child relocating, and you wish to object to the move as a whole, then the Court will have to consider this along with the other issues.

As with any application for an Order under Section 8 of the Children Act 1989, the welfare of the child is the paramount consideration. The Court will need to determine this in line with the Welfare Checklist. The quality of the school is a significant consideration. However, there are other factors, as set out below, which you should consider when drafting any witness statements within the proceedings:

◆ Will the parent with care of the child be able to make arrangements for the child to be taken to and collected from school on time?

◆ Are there other good reasons for a child to attend a particular school; for example, do they have siblings and an established friendship group they would benefit from attending school with?

◆ Is there a specific aspect to the school that is of particular importance; for example, if your child has mobility difficulties, is one school more suitable in terms of stairs or modifications?

◆ When seeking to argue for a particular school, you may therefore find it useful to answer the following questions:

   ◆ What is it about the school that makes it the best choice for your child?

   ◆ For example, does it have a reputation for good-quality teaching in a particular field?

◆ Will the child be able to pursue a particular interest to a high level, or is there an important peer group that the child needs to remain a part of?

Will the child be able to attend the school? Are there places?

You may need to contact the school and negotiate to keep a place open pending your application being decided.

How does attending this school fit with your child's routine?

◆ Will travelling to or from the school unnecessarily prolong your child's school day?

◆ You may need to look into travelling times from your child's address, collection and routes for public transport and school buses. Is there an early breakfast club, or an after-school club they can attend, if need be?

◆ How would that additional provision be funded? If you are not the parent the child lives with during the week, are you able to contribute to the costs of any travel or out of hours provision?

◆ Will attending that particular school mean the child can continue with their established activities?

Is the proposed school a fee-paying school?

◆ If so, how will the fees be paid?

◆ Can the Court be confident that the fees can be maintained to keep the place within the school stable?

Is this the first time a child has moved school?

The Court is likely to avoid repeated changes of school for a child as this may affect their overall education.

What stage is the child at in their education?

Changing schools midway through a GCSE course, or other crucial stage in a child's education, is something that the Court would need good reason to order.

What time of year is the proposed move?

◆ it is often more preferable to allow a child to complete a term or half term at a school and change schools after a holiday than to change midway through a term;

◆ it is important to think through when you intend to make an application and the effect it will have on the child;

◆ applications to court can take their time to resolve so you need to think in terms of not only the date you start your application but also in terms of how long it may take the Court to decide the case.

Ideally, the witness statements and evidence you produce to the Court will cover all significant issues such as those outlined above.

It can also be helpful for you to visit and research the schools proposed by the other side. This is important because, again, the Court expects parents to try to agree things between themselves in the first place and if both parents visit each other's schools it can help the parties to narrow the issues. If you have visited the other party's proposed schools and still disagree, it can help you to consider your reasons why.

CAFCASS

CAFCASS is the Children and Family Courts Advisory and Support Service. They have responsibility, when asked, to conduct safeguarding checks and investigate welfare issues. Their role is discussed further in Chapter 12.

CAFCASS may or may not be required to give an opinion. If the issue of schooling is just part of a wider application, such as for contact or for a child to live with a parent, then it is likely that a CAFCASS report will be ordered and the reporting officer may be able to comment. The child's wishes and feelings' report could be helpful to allow the Court to understand the views of the child concerned but if the child is very young, this is unlikely to be helpful because the Court has to look at the wishes of the child *in the light of his or her age and understanding.* With very young children, it is likely that parents would make the decision about schooling on behalf of the child. The older a child gets, the more they may be consulted but once the application is before the Court, unless the parties can agree and settle the case, the decision is one for the Judge.

It is important to consider carefully whether you think a report would assist. One of the advantages is that it gives the Court an independent opinion. One of the disadvantages is that it takes time to prepare a CAFCASS report and this can make it more difficult to keep school places open.

9

Applying to Change a Child's Name

This is another area in which the Court can make decisions. Firstly, the Court can be asked to make a Specific Issue Order to the effect that a child's name shall be changed, or a Prohibited Steps Order can be asked for to prevent a child's name being changed.

CONSULTING THE OTHER PARENT

If you intend to change the name of your child, you need to consult the other parent. Even if that parent does not have Parental Responsibility, the Court is likely to consider that this should be done and you could be criticised for changing the name without any notice.

There is case law to say that even where the father does not have Parental Responsibility, the child's name should not be changed without agreement or Order.

Whether your application is to change the name of the child officially or just informally by, for example, asking teachers to use a different name at school, you should consult the other parent. You can only change a child's birth certificate by Court Order or a deed poll. The deed poll is a separate document a Solicitor can help you with if the change of name is agreed.

Forenames

How the Court will approach any application will depend on the facts of the case and also the reasons for the proposed change. It is extremely uncommon to change a child's first name. A Christian name given to a child on baptism can be changed on confirmation, by Act of Parliament or at the time of adoption. That said, it is very common for children to be known by different first names, be it through shortening their names from, for instance, Natasha to Tasha or from Richard to Rich. It is also not uncommon for children to be known by nicknames or 'given names'.

Surnames

The change of surname is however an area of law that has brought much litigation in recent years, with the leading cases being Dawson v Wearmouth [1999] 2WLR 960 and Re W, Re A, Re B (Change of Name) [1999] 2FLR 933.

The reasons for changing a child's surname are usually to reflect the child's family background. If a father is not registered on the birth certificate, the child may have been registered using the mother's surname. It can be the case that the father then seeks to change the surname as part of any contact application. Simply to change the child's surname to match those of half-siblings does not, however, usually carry a lot of weight.

It can also be the case that a mother may apply to change the child's surname to her new married name in order that the child's surname is the same as, for example, half-siblings the child may have.

The question of a change of name can be a very emotional one and it is important to think carefully before making any application to the Court. Such applications are not always successful. It will very much depend on the circumstances of the case.

WHAT WILL THE COURT CONSIDER?

The starting point for the Court in deciding whether to allow a change of surname is the Welfare Principle and Checklist. There are also a number of other considerations, which the Court will take into account in any such application.

The Court should not permit a change of name unless it has evidence that it would improve the child's welfare. The Court should also consider the registered surname of the child and the reason for the registration, for instance to maintain a biological link with the father. The Court will consider the effect of the change of surname on the child both now and in the future. If one side changed the surname without permission, the reason for the change will be considered.

Any change of circumstances of the child since the original registration may be relevant.

Where the parents were married to each other, the fact of the marriage is important and it would normally take strong reasons for the Court to change the name from the father's surname if the child was so registered.

If the child's parents were not married to each other, the mother has control over registration. Consequently, on an application to change the surname of the child, the degree of commitment of the father to the child, the quality of contact, if it occurs, between father and child, the existence or absence of PR will all be relevant factors to take into account.

If the proposed change is to ensure the child's security and protection then this could be a reason to allow a change.

How do I apply?

The way of applying to the Court is the same for any specific issue or Prohibited Steps Order, or under Section 13 of the Children Act. As set out above, it starts with a Form C100 or a C2 depending on whether you are in court proceedings already.

Do CAFCASS need to prepare a report?

CAFCASS could be asked to prepare an s. 7 report on this issue. The views of the school may be helpful to the application. The wishes and feelings of the child may well be a relevant factor, particularly with older children. It is highly unlikely that a child will be required to be known under a new name against their wishes.

Double-barrelled surnames

Double-barrelled surnames can be a useful compromise in cases where a parent seeks to include their surname for the child, as can adopting a parent's surname as a middle name. This can be done by consent or asked for in the Court Order.

Step-parent or a new partner

In cases involving changing the name to include that of a step-parent, there are other issues that will require serious consideration such as the wishes and feelings of the child, the longevity of the new relationship and the position of the parent responding to the application.

10

Representing Yourself in Court

ADDRESSING THE JUDGE

The significance of using the correct form of address is that it shows the Court appropriate respect. If you find in the hearing that you become nervous and struggle to remember the correct address, do not forget you will be able to hear what the other side calls the Judge, which can be helpful, particularly if they are legally represented. If you make a genuine mistake, do not worry about it. The main point is that you should be polite and calm.

OBSERVING COURT ETIQUETTE

It is court etiquette that requires you to stand whenever a Judge or Magistrate leaves or enters the room.

It is also polite not to wear hats in court, and not to eat, chew gum or drink anything other than the water provided in the courtroom.

Proceedings are usually tape recorded in order that there is an accurate record of what is said, particularly if there is to be any appeal.

Make sure you take the case papers with you. Do not expect the Court to provide you with papers on the day. You could be disadvantaged if you do not have your papers but the other side and the Judge do have papers. You cannot assume a case will be adjourned if you did not bring the relevant papers with you. If a case is adjourned for that reason, there is a risk that you will be ordered to pay the costs of the hearing that had to be adjourned.

TYPES OF COURTROOM

The types of courtroom you will be in will depend on the type of Judge you are in front of. Where you sit, and how you address the Court, will depend on the room you are in.

Before Magistrates

When you appear before Magistrates, the usual arrangements are that the three magistrates will be sitting in a row at one end of the courtroom. Sitting in front of the Magistrates will be their Legal advisor. Legal advisors are qualified lawyers who are there to advise the Magistrates on the law.

It is usual for lawyers and parties to sit at desks facing the Magistrates. There will be a separate place for witnesses to come to give their evidence, called the witness box. It is not usual for you to have to stand up to speak to the Magistrates but it is always useful to check this with the Usher. You will usually address the chair of the Magistrates and it will only be the chair or their legal advisor that will speak to you. In a bench of three Magistrates, you should address the chair as 'Sir' or 'Madam'. It is not unusual to hear them referred to as 'Your Worships'.

District Judges

District Judges will often sit in their 'Chambers'. These rooms are usually relatively small; the Judge will be seated at a desk in the room and a large table will be set out for the lawyers and parties to sit at. The Judge is likely to be seated in their room when the case is called on and it is unusual for there to be a clerk or usher in the room. You should address them as 'Sir' or 'Madam'.

Circuit Judges

These Judges will appear in a courtroom in which they will sit at an elevated desk at one end of the courtroom. They will usually have at least one clerk sitting in front of them to assist with any administrative queries and their usher may also be in court. You should address the Judge as 'Your Honour'.

District Judges can also sit in a courtroom with the same layout.

The seating in front of the Judge will be arranged in rows. Lawyers and parties representing themselves will be on the front row, with clients sitting in the second row. If you are representing yourself then you should sit in the front row. There will be a witness box for people to give evidence from.

BEING AGAINST A LAWYER AT COURT

It is not unusual for cases to take place where one party is represented and one party is not. If you find yourself up against a lawyer, the following points are useful to remember:

◆ If the other side is legally represented, it is highly unlikely that you will be able to speak to them directly. You should expect to have your discussions with their lawyer.

◆ The Court would usually expect parties to discuss the case outside court, whether they are legally represented or not. Nobody is going to force you to have discussions with the other side's lawyer but it can be useful. You may be able to reach an agreement outside court without requiring the Judge to make a decision, for example. You may be able to learn a bit more about the arguments that the other side intend to present and you may be able to explain parts of your case that will help them to advise their client that a particular part of their case is not likely to succeed.

INTERIM HEARINGS

Clearly, preparing a case, obtaining evidence and CAFCASS reports can all take time and a Final Hearing in a family case can take a long time to arrive. There may be times during proceedings when a decision needs to be taken that cannot await the Final Hearing. We call hearings to decide such issues 'interim hearings'.

Examples of these sort of decisions might be:

◆ The Court is asked to consider whether a child should spend time with a parent before a Final Hearing. If the child lives with the mother, the mother may be objecting to the father spending unsupervised time with the child and this issue will need to be decided at a Final Hearing. However, the father may wish to spend supervised time with the child before this Final Hearing happens. There is nothing to stop the Court from making an interim decision as long as it is justified on the facts of the case and it does not pre-judge any issues the Court has decided should go to a Final Hearing.

◆ The parents of a child are in proceedings to argue about contact but they also do not agree which school the child ought to attend.

The end of the academic year is coming up and a decision needs to be taken about the child's school. The Court is not ready to decide contact yet. The Court can be asked to decide the question of a child's school as a stand alone hearing within proceedings.

◆ A parent with whom the child lives wishes to take the child out of England and Wales for a holiday. There are ongoing court proceedings for contact and the proposed holiday will mean that some contact dates are missed. The other parent objects to the changes. The Court can be asked to look at the issue of holidays and variations to contact before the Final Hearing.

One of the main questions to consider when asking for an interim hearing is whether asking the Court to make the interim decision will pre-judge any Final Hearing. For example, if a parent seeks unsupervised contact to a child and CAFCASS are preparing a report on this issue, there would be very little that could be achieved by also having an interim hearing on this point because the Court is likely to say that until the report is prepared, a decision cannot be made. It is important to be realistic about the purpose of any interim hearing.

Preparing for interim hearings, including the use of witness statements, will be no different to that of a Final Hearing (see page 147). There will still be the principle that parties disclose their evidence before any hearing and the rules of giving evidence do not change.

The First Hearing/Dispute Resolution Appointment
This is very often the first hearing you will attend at court. By the time this hearing takes place, you should have:

- attended a MIAM or have been told you are exempt;

- spoken to CAFCASS for your initial discussion;

- received the Safeguarding Checks.

You will by now have some idea of what the issues will be in your case, and also what the other side is going to be saying.

The CAFCASS recommendations in the safeguarding letter are going to be particularly important as this will be something the Court needs to consider.

The purpose of the first hearing is to allow the Court to plan the rest of the case. If you can reach a final agreement at that hearing, then that is clearly very helpful as the case can be concluded.

If not, this hearing will need to consider whether there is a need for any further involvement from CAFCASS (such as a Section 7 Report – see Chapter 12), whether there is any need for expert evidence and whether there can be some contact in the meantime.

Where there are any allegations of domestic violence or other harm then these will also be considered and a decision may then be made as to whether there needs to be a Finding of Fact Hearing.

It is unlikely that you will be giving evidence at that first hearing. What you will need to do instead is to think carefully about your case, the things you want the Court to look at and the steps you will ask the Court to take. Be prepared to compromise. Unlike a mediation appointment, however, what you say is not protected.

What is said in court can be referred to later and so make sure that you offer things that you feel comfortable with and will be prepared to stick to. Remember to take a pen and paper with you to court (or a computer) so that you can take a detailed note of what is said and done. You will receive a copy of the Order, which the Court makes either at the time or after the hearing, but your own note can also prove very helpful.

The hearing may not be listed for very long but it will be expected that there are discussions outside court.

Do not assume your case will be heard on time, or take only the hour or thirty minutes it has been allocated. You should be prepared to attend court in good time, ideally an hour before the time it is to be heard, and be prepared to stay all day.

Contact, perhaps at a contact centre, may be discussed and it is very useful to find out in advance where your local centres are, when they can start contact and confirm how much it costs. You can ask CAFCASS for this information.

DISPUTE RESOLUTION HEARING

This is an important hearing and takes place at the point when:

- any Finding of Fact Hearing has taken place and the facts found are known;

- any CAFCASS report has been received and considered;

- any experts' reports have been received.

It is not necessarily the case that your final witness statement will have been written. The purpose of this hearing is to allow you to try to reach an agreement in your case before there is to be a Final Hearing. Any Final Hearing should be seen as a last resort. They are stressful and difficult and they put you in the position of having to perhaps say difficult and unpleasant things to the other parent. Whatever the outcome of any Final Hearing, you will still have to work with the other parent and a Final Hearing can do a lot of damage to your ability to do that.

By the time the Dispute Resolution Hearing takes place, you will know what the experts are saying, and therefore which aspect of your case (and the other side's!) are likely to succeed. You can use this information to help you negotiate.

If you cannot reach an agreement, the case will need a Final Hearing. The Dispute Resolution Hearing will be your opportunity to decide what other steps you want to be taken before this happens and which witnesses you will want.

Before you attend this hearing, it is a good idea to read and re-read the reports carefully. Make a note of any points you want to challenge at a Final Hearing. This is not with a view to telling the Court all about them at the Dispute Resolutions Hearing but to help you decide which witnesses you will want to call to give evidence. If you want to challenge what someone is saying, you are very likely to need them to give evidence. It will also help you to work out your best points for negotiation.

Decide what you think you can realistically negotiate at the hearing and think carefully about whether you would be able to accept that. Remember, at a Final Hearing the outcome will be harder to predict. If you push a case to a Final Hearing, although you could come away with what you would like, there is equally a chance that you could come away with less than you like. You may feel that negotiating an arrangement that you can live with is a safer option.

Dispute Resolution Hearings are not lengthy appointments on paper. They may be listed for only an hour or half an hour. Much as with the first hearing, however, you can expect that there is likely to be much discussion outside court and you should prepare to be at court all day if need be.

FURTHER CASE MANAGEMENT DIRECTIONS

These hearings are only needed where there is either an unforeseen reason to bring the case back to court, or where there is a need to come back to court before a Finding of Fact Hearing or dispute resolution appointment because there is a need to give consideration to new information.

It may be, for example, that at a first hearing there is a question as to whether a Finding of Fact Hearing is needed because it is alleged that a parent drinks too much alcohol. There may be many allegations of domestic violence. It may be that a hair-strand test is ordered at the first hearing, and the parents ordered to set out further details about the domestic violence allegations. It is then that a Further Case Management Hearing will be 'listed' (i.e. set up on a particular date) to look at the outcome of the hair-strand test and to decide if there is going to be a Finding of Fact Hearing.

An example of an unforeseen need to bring the case back to court may be if contact at a particular contact centre is agreed, but that centre has no space to start contact and the parents cannot agree where contact should take place. You can ask for a Further Case Management Hearing by making an application using Form C2. It is always helpful to try to agree a way forward before going to the expense of a further court hearing.

Not every case will need a Further Case Management Directions Hearing.

COSTS

The Courts have historically not wanted the threat of costs to discourage parents from making applications in relation to seeing their children or determining issues about their children. As such, costs Orders in family cases are very unusual, but it is possible for a Judge to order a party to pay the costs of a case. This can be for one hearing, or for more than one. The law actually says that the Judge is able to make whatever Order he or she considers just.

The main reason for ordering a party to pay costs is whether they have behaved in a way that is unreasonable. Just because someone is not successful in their case does not automatically mean that they have been unreasonable.

You can be ordered to pay costs if, for example, you do not comply with court directions. If you do not file a statement by the time you have been ordered to, this can mean that people replying to your statement cannot file their evidence on time and this can mean that court hearings have to be adjourned. If this happens, and you did not have a good reason for failing to file a statement, you can be asked to pay the other side's costs of the hearing. This can be a significant amount of money.

Just because you may not be able to afford to pay costs, it does not mean you won't be ordered to pay anything. The Court will give you a chance to make arguments as to whether you should pay costs and how much. This may take place on a later date.

The Court does not have to make an Order for costs even if you prove there has been unreasonable behaviour. The Court can take into account all the circumstances of the case. This can include considerations such as the effect that making a party pay costs will have on the parent's ability to cooperate in the future.

11

Domestic Violence

INJUNCTIONS

This book is intended to cover applications in children cases. However, applications for Non-Molestation and Occupation Orders can have an effect on children proceedings and so it is important to explain what they are and when the Court will grant one.

It can be the case that when a relationship ends and there are allegations of domestic violence, one of the parties may try to obtain a Non-Molestation Order and/or an Occupation Order. Not every case of domestic violence requires one of these Orders and just because a party did not apply for one does not mean that they cannot raise domestic violence allegations in children cases.

These Orders are designed to protect victims of domestic abuse from a violent partner. They are serious Court Orders and it is important that you try to get some advice if this happens in your case.

NON-MOLESTATION ORDERS

Non-Molestation Orders are granted to protect the 'health, safety and well being' of the person applying for them. They can include terms such as preventing the person named in the Order from using or threatening violence against them, threatening or harassing them, or even more specific things such as not sending them messages on Facebook. They can also prevent the person named in the Order from going within a particular distance of certain addresses, or prevent them from contacting the person who applied for the Order in any way, except through Solicitors.

OCCUPATION ORDERS

Occupation Orders are granted to manage the occupation of the family home. This can include requiring a person to leave, requiring the person in the property to allow the other person back in, and directing how the house may be occupied (for example, lived in by one person at weekends and by one person in the week).

They are different applications to the Court from the applications about children, although it is possible for children to be named in the Orders. Both a Non-Molestation Order and an Occupation Order are covered by the Family Law Act 1996.

You can apply for a Non-Molestation Order against someone the Court would describe as an 'associated person'. This includes people who have been in an intimate personal relationship with each other, that is or was of significant duration.

Non-Molestation and Occupation Orders can be made by the Court without giving notice to the person who is going to be affected by it. The Court will do this where a good reason is given; for example, if the person applying is afraid what will happen to them if the other side is told in advance that an injunction is being sought.

If you have been served with one of these Orders after a hearing you were not told about, then it is important that you remember three things.

Firstly, you are bound by the Order made unless and until the Court varies it. This is the case even if you have just been told that the Order has been made, but have not been given a copy of it.

Secondly, you are entitled to ask for a hearing to ask the Court to reconsider the decision if one hasn't already been set.

Thirdly, whatever decision the Court has made at the without notice hearing, it will not be a final decision. The Court will have heard one side of the story and will have had to make a decision based on that evidence. Do not assume that the Court will have already made up its mind. You are entitled to bring evidence and challenge the Order if that is what you choose to do.

RELEVANCE OF DOMESTIC VIOLENCE TO CHILDREN CASES

Domestic violence or abuse, even in cases where it was limited to violence between the parents, can be relevant in deciding whom a child lives with and whom they spend time with. This is because, when looking at such questions, the Court has to consider the Welfare Checklist, which includes any harm the child has suffered or is at risk of suffering. If there are questions about whether a parent has anger management issues or drug or alcohol problems, it can be important to investigate those before that parent has unsupervised time with their child, to make sure their child is kept safe.

This may be the case even when the parent concerned denies domestic violence. If it is a live question in the case (i.e. if the allegations are serious, relevant and being used as a reason to limit the child's time with that person), the Court is likely to be unwilling to order unsupervised time until there has been a trial to decide whether the allegations of abuse are true.

CAFCASS is likely to express an opinion about the relevance of any allegations of violence as part of the safeguarding checks, but the ultimate decision is for the Court.

Domestic violence does not always mean that a parent shall never see their child. It may well mean instead that any time that parent spends with their child will need to be monitored and steps taken to make sure the child is safe.

Contact can be supervised, either in a professional setting or by a trusted relative. CAFCASS can refer violent partners to a Domestic Violence Perpetrators Programme which is a very intensive course designed to educate perpetrators on the effect of domestic abuse on children. Other risk assessments are possible.

One of the key issues in any case where domestic violence is admitted or proved is looking at how much the perpetrator accepts what they have done and how much remorse they show. Someone who fully understands what they have done wrong is less likely to reoffend.

Cases where relevant domestic violence or abuse is alleged are different to other children cases because there are extra safety considerations. The steps to decide such cases usually go like this:

◆ What are the allegations?

◆ Are the allegations, if proved, relevant to contact?

◆ Are the allegations denied or accepted?

◆ Does there need to be a separate trial (Finding of Fact Hearing) to decide the allegations before the case can be finally decided?

◆ What time, if any, can the child spend with the parent in the meantime?

◆ If there doesn't need to be a separate trial, does there need to be a CAFCASS risk assessment or other report to help decide the issues?

◆ If there is a separate trial, have the allegations been proved?

◆ If there is a separate trial, does the judgment of that trial mean that there needs to be a CAFCASS risk assessment or other report to help decide the issues?

◆ What work does the person found to have been violent need to do?

◆ What Order is now in the best interests of the child?

FINDING OF FACT HEARINGS

A Finding of Fact Hearing is usually an interim hearing where evidence is heard by the Court to determine whether there was domestic violence in the relationship or to the child. The Court will consider any such allegations and come to a determination.

The process for a Finding of Fact Hearing is very similar to that of the Final Hearing, but with two important exceptions.

Firstly, whereas the party who goes first in any Final Hearing is the person applying for the Order, the party who goes first in a Finding of Fact Hearing is the person making the allegations. That is because the person making the allegations needs to set out their case, so that the person responding can reply knowing everything that is being said against them.

Secondly, whereas a Final Hearing will result in a Final Order, it is highly likely that the case will continue after the Finding of Fact Hearing and so you will need to think about what you would like the Court to do once it has decided whether the allegations have been proved.

There is still evidence in chief (see page 191), cross-examination and the chance for re-examination. You will also need to do a closing argument.

One useful document for any Finding of Fact Hearing is a Scott Schedule (see page 124). This is the list of allegations made and the replies to them. You can use this document to help structure your questions and also your submissions.

When the Court is asked to decide whether a Finding of Fact Hearing is necessary, the Judge may also decide which of the allegations in the case are to be heard in that hearing. It is not uncommon for you to be asked to set out all of your allegations before the Court decides if a Finding of Fact Hearing is necessary.

The Court can select which allegations it wants to hear evidence about. It will decide this based on what is the most relevant.

It can be difficult to deal with allegations of domestic abuse or other harm when you represent yourself and if the Court makes findings against you this will have consequences for your case. If you are in certain professions, such as the Police, teaching or medical, they can also have consequences for your job. The findings made will stand unless you are able to successfully appeal them (see Chapter 17 below).

This means that the Court will treat you as having been guilty of the matters that were proved against you, even if you do not accept that the Court got it right. The success of your application could depend on your willingness to accept what the Court has found and its ability to put it right (for example, through anger management or the CAFCASS-organised Domestic Violence Perpetrator Programmes).

Similarly, if you are the one making allegations and you do not succeed in proving them, the Court will proceed as though the allegations did not happen. This can mean, for example, that the other side moves quickly to unsupervised time with the child.

If you are found to have lied in proceedings, and been prepared to make false allegations, then this will also affect the way the Court deals with your case.

It therefore follows that a Finding of Fact Hearing is an extremely important hearing. Even if you intend to conduct your case without legal representation on the whole, it would be very sensible to consider getting representation for a Finding of Fact Hearing.

The issues raised by Finding of Fact Hearings can be very personal and unpleasant. Without a legal representative, you would be required to cross-examine alone on these highly sensitive matters.

Sometimes it is possible for Finding of Fact Hearings to resolve without the need for evidence. This tends to happen where the parties are able to agree what is and is not relevant to the issues, and concessions are offered. Someone facing a number of allegations of violence, for example, may be prepared to accept that a limited number happened, which would mean that having a hearing about the few that are not admitted may not be needed. If you enter into these negotiations at court, it is important to remember that you will be taken to have done everything you admit to, and so only accept as much as you are comfortable with. It is also important to make a careful note of what it is you have agreed to. This will usually be put before the Court and it will be up to the Judge if there needs to be a hearing on any allegations not agreed.

When you give evidence, unless the Court decides to the contrary, you will do it in a courtroom in the presence of all parties and any lawyers acting on their behalf. Sometimes people come to give evidence who are particularly vulnerable. If a person is alleging serious domestic violence, for example, and the other side is not legally represented, they could be expected to be cross-examined by the very person they say abused them.

SPECIAL MEASURES

The Court does have the power in the right circumstances to put in place 'special measures' to allow a vulnerable witness to give evidence. This can include giving evidence via a video link or from behind a screen.

It is up to the person who wants the special measures to ask for them in advance of the hearing they are to give evidence at. It is an application you can oppose; however, it is important to remember that the Court sees special measures as a neutral step. Just because someone is given special measures does not mean that what they are saying will be viewed as more plausible and the Judge will bear that in mind.

ALLEGING DOMESTIC VIOLENCE

These sorts of allegations are serious and it is worth considering again whether you are eligible for Legal Aid, or if you can get any sort of legal advice, particularly if you think you need the protection of an injunction.

Examples

Mrs Smith alleges that Mr Smith assaulted his ex-wife ten years ago and he is now having an affair with Mrs Smith's best friend. She does not think that their children should spend time with him. Mr Smith denies the assault ten years ago and he insists his new relationship started after he separated from Mrs Smith.

This type of case is unlikely to require a Finding of Fact Hearing. The allegation of violence is old, there are no allegations that he was violent during this marriage. The fact that he has a new relationship is not a factor that requires a separate hearing for the Court to consider. A new relationship is unlikely to prevent any contact between a parent and their children or to require contact to take place under any special conditions unless there is evidence that the new partner is a safeguarding risk.

> *Miss Jones alleges that Mr Brown used to drink alcohol to excess during their relationship, including after the birth of their daughter, and when he was drunk, he used to be physically abusive. She ended the relationship six months ago and does not want there to be any unsupervised contact between Mr Brown and his daughter. Mr Brown denies any allegation of wrongdoing and sees no reason why he cannot have his daughter stay with him every other weekend.*

This case is likely to require a Finding of Fact Hearing. The allegations are recent and relevant. Even though Miss Jones is not saying that Mr Brown should not spend any time with his child, the parties clearly disagree as to how this should happen. CAFCASS alone will not be able to resolve this dispute of fact and so the Court may well see the benefit in dealing with the factual issues at an early stage, particularly before referring it to CAFCASS for a report.

> *Mrs Wilson alleges that Mr Wilson was violent to her on many occasions throughout their four-year marriage. Mr Wilson accepts that he did use violence on five occasions during the marriage, he is very sorry for this and he will attend anger management. He accepts that on three of those occasions he received a Police Caution or a conviction in the Magistrates Court. He denies any of the other incidents Mrs Wilson says happened.*

Although the allegations are recent and relevant, it is not inevitable that the Court will order a Finding of Fact Hearing. Mr Wilson clearly accepts some physical violence and the Court may consider that there is enough information to go on. However, if the allegations Mr Wilson accepts are much less serious than the ones alleged, the Court may still consider that it is necessary to examine those issues in a Finding of Fact Hearing. Mr Wilson's criminal convictions (including cautions) will be proof in the Family Court of violence.

APPLYING FOR CHILD ARRANGEMENTS ORDERS IN DOMESTIC VIOLENCE CASES AND WHEN TO RAISE DOMESTIC VIOLENCE

Make sure that you set out your allegations clearly when you are given the chance to (on Form C100 or the response form).

You may well find it helpful to write down for your own benefit at an early stage what you say happened, with reference to particular dates (if you can) and notes on who was present for each incident.

If your ex-partner has a criminal conviction, or a caution for assaulting you, you will not need to prove that incident all over again because criminal convictions are admissible in the Family Court. If, however, your ex-partner was found not guilty, you are not prevented from making that allegation again in the Family Court because it works in a different way to the Criminal Court. Cautions count as criminal convictions.

Whenever you make an allegation that is denied by the other side it is for you to prove on the 'balance of probabilities' that it happened. The 'balance of probabilities' is sometimes written as proving an allegation so the Court feels it is 'more likely than not' that it occurred. It is not the same as a criminal allegation, which must be proved 'beyond reasonable doubt'. Think about a set of scales. If they balance in favour of one side, even to a small degree, then that side succeeds.

You will be required at some stage to set your allegations out in a 'Scott Schedule'. This is a specific form of document that is used to show the Court what the issues are. It is a table with four columns.

In the first column, the date of each incident is given.

In the second column, brief details of each incident alleged are set out, and the incidents are cross-referenced to pages in the court bundle.

In the third column, the other side writes their response to the incident and adds their own cross-referencing to the court bundle.

The fourth column is left blank for the Court to complete as decisions are made.

You will need to provide the evidence you are relying on. Sometimes there are no other witnesses to domestic abuse other than the perpetrator. You will not be prevented from relying on important, relevant allegations just because there are no other witnesses; however the Court will have to take that into account when deciding what happened.

Similarly, just because you may not be able to remember the precise dates everything happened this will not mean you are prevented from relying on an allegation, especially if it was a long time ago. The Court is less likely to hear allegations that are very old, unless they are serious or particularly relevant. If you cannot remember the exact date of an incident, just be as accurate as you can. Try to remember, for example, the time of year, how old your children were, which address you were living at or whether anything specific triggered the incident, which would help you to date it.

The Court is more likely to allow evidence from witnesses who saw an incident or its immediate aftermath than from witnesses who perhaps didn't see anything but who simply dislike the other side. The key is to keep your case as clear and as relevant as possible.

RESPONDING TO ALLEGATIONS OF DOMESTIC VIOLENCE

When you are responding to allegations of domestic violence, the first thing to remember is that the 'burden of proof' is on the person making the allegations. Just as a person is innocent until proven guilty in the Criminal Court, the same applies in the Family Court. You will, however, still need to respond to the case against you.

The Court will be most interested in evidence that is relevant to the allegations against you. You need to give your side of the story to each of the incidents. You will need to think about whether there were any witnesses to what happened, or who can support your version of events before or after the event complained about.

If, for example, it is said that you assaulted your ex-partner when guests were staying in the house, would any of those guests remember the visit? Did your ex-partner seem upset to them or not? Did they see any injures or not? Do you have any photographs of that particular weekend?

If you have any admissions to make, make them early. If you have acted in a way that was wrong, you can often do far more to help your case by admitting this at an early stage and taking steps to deal with it before waiting until the last possible moment, after the Court has already found you responsible.

A letter of apology, or a statement setting out what you accept you have done and how sorry you feel, may go some way towards establishing that you have genuine remorse, together with a willingness to undertake work around domestic violence. If you have already done this work, provide proof. Do you have a conviction for domestic violence and, if so, can your probation officer provide any information about what you have done? Did your behaviour come at a time when you were drinking to excess or using drugs? Have you addressed that now? Can you provide a letter from a support worker or your doctor setting this out?

Have Social Services been involved since that time with your children and have they said anything about the risk you pose?

These are all useful things to consider when approaching questions of domestic violence and contact.

POLICE EVIDENCE

The Police keep logs of all call-outs to their area going back over a long time. The Court can ask the Police to produce records of incidents between partners if it is relevant to the matter in court. It is always possible for the Police to raise an objection to this if, for example, there is intelligence in their files that they do not want disclosed to the parties in court – but in practice this is very rare.

CAFCASS can also obtain information from the Police as part of their safeguarding checks but they will not receive full copies of all Police logs.

The type of information the Police will have for call-outs is as follows:

Call-out logs – written accounts of the calls received from the victim and between Police units responding to an incident.

Pocket book – notes taken by individual Police Officers in their notebooks.

Witness statements – any statements taken by the Police in their investigations.

Record of interview – if a person was arrested and interviewed, the Police will have a copy of the interview tapes and also a typed record of the interview. The Police may be reluctant to produce copies of the tape recordings themselves without guarantees being signed to cover their safe storage and proper use. If the allegations involved children or other vulnerable witnesses in any way, then they are likely to have been interviewed on a DVD. Again, the Police will be reluctant to provide these without being assured that they will be kept safe.

When requesting that the Police disclose information, it can help to give as much detail as possible about the people they are being asked to disclose information about. This includes, but is not limited to, full names, relevant addresses and dates of birth. If an address is to be kept confidential, make sure the Order asks for that to be done. It is also useful to give the Police dates for the disclosure. 'Any incidents involving Mr X (date of birth 5.5.1975) and Mrs Y (date of birth 6.6.1976) at the address of 1 High Street, London or 12 Main Street, Milton Keynes between August 2010 and January

2014' is likely to be much easier to comply with than 'any incidents involving Mr X and Mrs Y'. The Police will need some time to comply with any Court Order for disclosure. Usually, Courts allow 28 days for this. It is also the case that the Police need to be given an opportunity to object to making the disclosure, if necessary.

If there has been a relevant criminal conviction, then the Probation Service in that criminal case may have been asked to prepare a pre-sentence report. This can be a useful document because it will include the outcome of any interview between the person convicted and the probation officer, together with the Probation Service's opinion on the level of risk posed by the person convicted. It can be useful for the Court to have this information.

If someone was sentenced for an offence and it is relevant, the comments made by the Judge who sentenced that person can also be obtained. This is done by asking the Criminal Court to provide a transcript for that hearing. There may be a small charge to get it and you will need to give as much detail about the time and date of the hearing as possible.

The Police and other agencies cannot provide information about people other than the parties to the case without their consent.

12

Understanding the Role of CAFCASS

CAFCASS stands for Children and Family Court Advisory and Support Service.

It is the largest employer of social workers in the country and is used by the Court specifically to provide expert professional advice on safeguarding issues in relation to children and families. They also give advice and recommendations about things that are in dispute between the parties. Their social workers can give evidence in court proceedings and, on occasion, represent the child in court proceedings.

It is the role of CAFCASS to look after the interests of children involved in family proceedings as they can often get lost between arguing parents. They will work with children and their families and then advise the Courts on what they consider to be in the best interests of children.

Although CAFCASS undertake work and write reports on behalf of the Court they are, strictly speaking, independent of the Court. They are also independent of Social Services, the Police, education and health authorities and all similar agencies.

Their role is therefore extremely important. In many ways they are the eyes and the ears of the Judge outside of the courtroom. They have the time and expertise to interview the parents, speak with the Local Authority, undertake basic background checks and also, if necessary, to meet with the children.

After conducting their initial investigations, CAFCASS will prepare a report to the Court (you will also get a copy of this report), which will also set out their recommendations on the issue that the Court is considering.

The CAFCASS report is so important to the outcome of the proceedings that it is sensible for you to have a good relationship with the author of that report. They do not come to the case with any preconceived views. Their role is completely impartial. You need to treat them with professionalism and respect. Return their calls promptly and also make sure you turn up on time fully prepared for any meetings that you have with them. Be honest with them. The last thing you want the Judge to read when considering the application is that you have been unhelpful, rude or belligerent with CAFCASS.

It is important to realise that they are not the enemy and a Judge will take their report very seriously. However, remember that in law a child has the right to have contact with its family unless there are specific questions about the child's safety. The law therefore is working towards the right outcome for the child.

The main types of cases in which the Courts ask CAFCASS for help are when there are questions about:

- where the child should live;

- whom the child should live with;

- whether the child should spend time with someone;

- what school the child should attend;

- whether the child should leave the country either on holiday or permanently;

- whether the child's surname should be changed.

HEARING FROM CAFCASS

Introductory letter

The first time you will hear from CAFCASS is after you or your ex-partner (or other family members) have made an application to the Court. They will write an introductory letter to you and the other party confirming that they have been asked by the Court to prepare a safeguarding report, which is often called a Schedule 2 letter. CAFCASS will write to both you and your ex-partner once they have received the papers to confirm that they are now acting in this matter and advise you to expect a telephone call from them.

The Schedule 2 letter

Whenever any Child Arrangements Order application is made to the Court, the Court will forward a copy to CAFCASS, who will undertake some initial safeguarding checks.

They will prepare a brief report, usually between two or three pages long, which is known as a Schedule 2 safeguarding letter. The Schedule 2 letter will deal with CAFCASS's safeguarding concerns and its recommendations for the next steps in the case.

The recommendation could be that there is no reason for CAFCASS to remain involved and invites the Court to make an Order as it sees fit, or it could ask the Court to allow it to undertake a full investigation and provide a detailed recommendation on the most appropriate way forward.

CAFCASS could make one or more of the following recommendations:

◆ that the Court should arrange for a Fact Finding Hearing;

◆ that one of the parties should undertake an alcohol test;

◆ that one of the parties should undertake a drugs test;

◆ that a child or children should spend time with a party;

◆ that a party should send age-appropriate letters, cards or small gifts to a child or children for a period of time;

◆ that both parties should undertake the Separated Parents Information Programme;

◆ that there needs to be enhanced information provided by the Police;

◆ that CAFCASS have such concerns that they would invite the Local Authority to be involved in the case as a matter of urgency.

SAFEGUARDING CHECKS

CAFCASS will contact Local Authorities and the Police in the areas in which you have been living during the past five years. They will be looking for information about any risks which your child or children have been exposed to. This information may relate to you, the children, or the other adults involved in your case. CAFCASS <u>do not</u> require the consent of any party before making these checks.

Examples of things that would be of interest to a CAFCASS officer are:

- whether the Police have been involved with the family and the extent of any involvement;

- whether the child has been the subject of Child Protection procedures such as a Child Protection Plan, a Child in Need Plan, Common Assessment Framework, Care Proceedings;

- whether there have been any reports of abuse within the family, e.g. physical, emotional or sexual abuse or neglect;

- whether the Local Authority has provided any support services to the family;

- whether there are any issues of alcohol use, drug use or domestic abuse within the family.

CAFCASS will speak with you

In most cases, a CAFCASS officer will call both you and your ex-partner. The CAFCASS officer will ask you both for information about your circumstances and about the child or children. The phone call is used to gather information, which can then be assessed and relayed to the Court. It is therefore important to be polite and cooperative.

This phone call will be made before the date of the first hearing and will usually be very close to the hearing date, so do not worry if you do not hear from them until immediately before the hearing.

It is not unusual to get the introductory letter from them and then not hear from them again until a telephone call the day before the first hearing. The call will normally last about 5–15 minutes and you will generally be asked about whether or not you support or oppose the application being made.

They may ask you:

◆ why the application has been made?

◆ what are the current arrangements in place for the children or child?

◆ whether you have any safeguarding concerns or issues about the other party. This may include, but is not limited to, issues of domestic abuse in the relationship (or afterwards), alcoholism or drug issues or any other concerns. It may also involve specific issues concerning the child or children.

Some advice

On receipt of the introductory letter, it is advisable to write down in a notebook the things that may concern you so that you do not forget anything when CAFCASS call you. If you have any concerns it is helpful if you set them out at the earliest opportunity.

In a small number of cases (usually when CAFCASS have received the application very close to the date set for the first hearing) they may not call you before the first hearing, but will have an officer at court who should be able to talk to you before your hearing. They may also talk to you at court before the hearing if they have not been able to reach you by phone.

CAFCASS will normally send a copy of the Schedule 2 letter to both parties before the first court hearing. However, if it contains sensitive information about one or more of the people involved in the court case CAFCASS may decide to send it only to the Court, so the Judge can decide whether to disclose all of the information to the parties.

If you do not receive a copy of the Schedule 2 letter before the first court hearing, do not worry. It is not unusual for the letter to only be ready on the day of the first court hearing and as such copies are usually provided at court.

If you are concerned that you have not had enough time to read the letter or take further advice then you must let the Court know at the hearing.

FIRST HEARING

At the first hearing the Schedule 2 letter will be given to the Judge and all parties. If this is not the case and the Schedule 2 letter has not been completed, then the Court will not be able to make any Order for the child to spend time with one of the parties. The Court needs to be sure that it is safe to make an Order and, without a Schedule 2 letter confirming that there are no safeguarding issues, the Court cannot make such an Order. This does not, however, prevent the parties while at court from agreeing between themselves for matters to be resolved or for a party to spend time with the child or children without the need for the Court's assistance by way of a formal Court Order.

On the day of the first court hearing there will be a duty CAFCASS Officer available at court to talk with all parties and obtain their views on the recommendation. It should be noted that CAFCASS officers will not be at court for any additional court hearings unless the Court formally orders their attendance. If, ultimately, a party decides to challenge a CAFCASS report (this may be the case with a Section 7 Report) then you will need to ask the Court to order their attendance for the Final Hearing.

If there are no safeguarding concerns the CAFCASS Officer will help to try and settle the matter between the parties.

If CAFCASS wish to undertake a detailed investigation before providing a recommendation they will discuss what can be done in the meantime to ensure that the child's best interests are met. This may mean that they will suggest the child spends some time with the parent either supervised in a contact centre, by a family friend or relative, or if appropriate, unsupervised time. If the child has not seen the party for some time then it may be suggested that there be a period where the time spent between the child and the party is organised in an indirect fashion. This may mean by an age-appropriate and child-focused card, letter or small present. It may also mean by telephone or Skype or FaceTime.

CONDUCTING A FULL INVESTIGATION

Section 7 Report

If CAFCASS seek to undertake a full investigation, the Court will usually allow them to do this. This will normally be recommended in the Schedule 2 letter and the Court will have to consider whether to order the report or not.

This investigation is known as a Section 7 Report. The Report will take around 12–14 weeks to be completed by CAFCASS. It will be prepared by a different CAFCASS officer from the one that either prepared the Schedule 2 letter or the one you met at court who tried to negotiate an agreement with you and the other party at the first appointment.

During this time, if necessary, extra information can be obtained from the Police, doctors, schools, Children's Services or any other appropriate person involved with the family. The CAFCASS Officer will usually have at least one meeting with each of the parents and any other relevant adults as he sees fit. Depending on the child's age they may also visit them or ask for them to be brought to the CAFCASS office to find out what the child's or children's views are. This meeting will be undertaken face to face between the CAFCASS officer and the child/children. Neither parent should be in the same room when this interview takes place, although with nervous children, parents can sometimes stay in the room to offer support. The CAFCASS officer will seek to understand the child's wishes and feelings as to the proposed Court Order, although it is not the role of the Court to dictate exactly how CAFCASS undertake their role.

If the Schedule 2 letter or the advice of the CAFCASS officer at court recommends the preparation of a Section 7 Report then the Court will usually agree. However, it will ask for your opinion and that of the other party. You will have to decide whether to agree or disagree. The principal reason people usually disagree is that it delays the final hearing. There is an argument that where the case is straightforward there may be little merit in waiting for CAFCASS to prepare an additional report. Remember, CAFCASS deals with welfare issues. If no welfare issues are identified and the main issue is the amount of time a parent spends with a child, then the Court may not need help from CAFCASS to decide this. While the CAFCASS Section 7 Report takes about 12–14 weeks to prepare, both parties will normally file some evidence (by way of witness statements) after they have received the reports before the matter gets listed for a Final Hearing. As such the instruction of an s.7 can delay the final determination by between 4–6 months.

Equally, if there is information outstanding and CAFCASS recommend the Section 7 Report then there may well be valid reasons for a report in this case. You will have to consider these arguments before coming to a decision whether to oppose or support the instruction. If you are unclear then you can ask the Court whether it is really necessary in light of the issues in dispute.

The scope of the Section 7 Report

The Court will decide what issues the Section 7 Report should consider. They will be set out in the Court Order so that everybody knows what the Section 7 Report is considering. For example, if your application is for you to be allowed to spend time with the child, then the report would seek to concentrate on that issue only. If, however, you are asking that the Court allows the child to live with you at your home and also seeking Parental Responsibility then the Court will invite CAFCASS to prepare the Section 7 Report on a number of issues. CAFCASS and the Court sometimes refer to this as a multi-issue report.

The law

The formal wording for this type of clause in a Court Order is as follows:

'CAFCASS to file and serve a Section 7 Report by 4pm on xx/xx/xxxx to deal with the issue of mother's/father's contact with the child George Washington (DOB 01.04.07)'

The phrase 'file and serve' means that CAFCASS must 'serve' or send a copy to both you and your opponent by the specific date and also 'file' or lodge a copy with the Court by the specific date.

It is not always the case that the CAFCASS report will be on time. If you have not received the report by the specified date then you should contact both CAFCASS and the Court to find out the reason for the delay. If there is a real problem, such as that CAFCASS have not received the Order or the officer is off sick, then it may be necessary to make an urgent application to the Court so that you can attempt to resolve the issue.

If the report is going to be just a few days late then this should not be too problematic. You may, however, have to amend the timetable with the other party. This can normally be done by a letter or email agreeing to a change in the dates so that both of you have time to file your witness statements and respond to the report. You should adopt a sensible and pragmatic approach under such circumstances. Where agreement cannot be reached and there is insufficient time to complete your witness statement, then you may need to apply to the Court for an extension by way of an urgent application.

The Local Authority can be asked to prepare a Section 7 Report

Where the Local Authority is involved or has been involved with safeguarding issues concerning the children or the parents, then the

Court will usually ask the Local Authority rather than CAFCASS to prepare the Section 7 Report. In this case it would normally be the child's social worker who would prepare the report.

For what type of issues does the Court order Section 7 Reports?

There are a number of issues that the Local Authority and/or CAFCASS could be instructed by the Court to consider when preparing a Section 7 Report, namely by way of example:

◆ where a child should live;

◆ whether the child's surname should be changed;

◆ what school the child should attend;

◆ whether a father should have Parental Responsibility;

◆ whether the child should spend time with a party;

◆ whether the time a child spends with a party should be supervised.

Preparing for the Section 7 Report

Part of the work that the CAFCASS officer will undertake when preparing the Section 7 Report will be to interview you.

You need to be clear and concise as to what you wish to tell the CAFCASS officer as to your view on the issue in dispute. The priority for the officer will be the child's welfare. The officer will expect you to prioritise the child in a sensible and balanced fashion and to be child focused. The officer will not expect you to be rude or aggressive towards them. Nor will they expect you to be difficult or uncooperative with regard to booking the appointment.

Do not be late and ensure that you can be at the meeting for as long as the officer needs. Do not book another appointment for immediately after the meeting with CAFCASS in case it overruns.

This is not an opportunity to 'character assassinate' the other party. CAFCASS will not be interested in certain matters, such as a failure to return goods after the relationship ended, that the ex was unfaithful or has refused to pay maintenance. In undertaking their investigation the officer will only really be concerned about matters of safeguarding and the Welfare Checklist.

They will be interested in domestic violence, domestic abuse and other safeguarding issues. They will be assisted where there is evidence of the above.

It is not uncommon for the some officers to negotiate between the two parties to try to resolve the dispute.

Prepare

- Draft for yourself a short note or aide memoire of the issues that you wish to discuss with the CAFCASS officer.

- Try to focus on the present and future, rather than the past.

- Be prepared to compromise.

- If spending time with the child is the issue, think about what time you or the other party should spend with the child and why for these specific times.

- If the other party is lying about something significant (such as saying you have never spent time with the child) and you can prove this lie (perhaps you have photos of yourself with the child) then it can be a good idea to have the proof to hand so that you can show the officer when you meet. This does, however, mean dredging up the past and stressing the other party's failings.

◆ Keep it simple and sensible.

◆ Be friendly, cooperative and child focused.

Make sure you have told the officer everything that you consider important. The last thing you want is for them to have left and you to have failed to tell them something important.

Despite the fact that CAFCASS officers only normally meet with a parent once (sometimes twice, depending on the officer's availability and resources), they will give you their telephone number or email address. If something happens during the course of their investigation or you change your mind or come to an agreement with the other side then you will still be able to contact them. Do not bombard them with insignificant information or try to become too friendly with them: use it only where necessary.

The Section 7 Report

Once the report is completed it will be sent out to both parties and a copy will be sent to the Court. From experience the report is normally between 6 and 10 pages long. It should set out the following:

◆ what work and investigations the CAFCASS officer has undertaken;

◆ the response of the family members to the current circumstances;

◆ a summary of the officer's social work assessment;

- whether the officer has spoken with the child/children, under what circumstances and what the child/children's wishes and feelings are;

- it should consider the Welfare Checklist as to the specific issue or issues which the Court has asked it to investigate and consider:

  - The officer's comments regarding the 'no order' principle and its relevance to this case;

  - the officer's analysis and recommendations.

You will then have the opportunity to consider the report prior to returning to court. If you agree with the analysis and recommendations of the report and the other party also agrees then it is likely that the matter can be resolved amicably at the next hearing without any argument or determination by the Court. Both parties would still need to attend the hearing and they should formalise a Final Order recording the agreement. Indeed, if there is only a minor disagreement as to something in the report then again this may well be something that can sensibly be agreed between you and the other party once you have both had an opportunity to consider the report and have a chat.

CHALLENGING THE CAFCASS REPORT

If you or the other party disagrees with the report then the matter would usually need to be listed for a contested Final Hearing, where both parties would give oral evidence. Normally the Court would list a Directions Hearing to consider matters after the CAFCASS report has been filed and served. If you or the other party disagrees with the report then you would need to ask the Court for the CAFCASS officer to attend the Final Hearing as follows:

> *'The author of the CAFCASS Section 7 Report dated xx/xx/*
> *xxxx, Ms Enid Blaydon, to attend the Final Hearing for the*
> *purposes of cross-examination.'*

It is very important that you seek an Order that the CAFCASS officer attend the Final Hearing if you do not agree with the recommendations. If the officer does not attend the Final Hearing then you cannot cross-examine the officer, which makes it extremely difficult to subsequently challenge their report or recommendations. You will need the opportunity for the officer to be cross-examined so that you can raise with them the errors that you consider in their report.

It is important to remember that the Court relies heavily on the CAFCASS officer to provide an independent assessment of the situation and ensure that the recommendations reflect what is in the interests of the child or children. As such the Court will normally follow the report's recommendations. The Court cannot depart significantly from its recommendations unless it has put its concerns or proposals to the CAFCASS officer and provided compelling reasons for doing so.

Despite the weight put on to their reports, it does not mean that their recommendations are always followed.

They may have got things factually wrong. This can happen. They may have misread a document from the Police or misunderstood something significant and then put considerable weight on that error in their analysis. Their analysis may have been completely different, if not for this factual error. This would be a good reason to challenge their report.

A spelling mistake or incorrect date of birth, while being a factual error, would not be grounds to challenge their report.

You may consider that they have not sufficiently explored one or more issues that you consider to be significant. The starting point is always to look at the Welfare Checklist and you may consider that they have not considered this appropriately or correctly. This is another good reason for challenging the report.

They may not have met with you or someone who is relevant to the case – for example, a new partner or an extended family member who may be offering you support to care for the child.

Another common complaint is about the interview that the officer has with the child or children. Ideally, depending on the child's age, this interview should be undertaken in a neutral venue, such as the school or the CAFCASS offices.

The officer is usually experienced in social work practice and familiar with speaking to children for the purpose of these reports. There is normally undertaken between the officer and the child a piece of work that consists of conversations and perhaps drawings. Neither parent should usually be in the room or within listening/ speaking distance of the child when the interview takes place. It is not normally ideal for more than one child to be interviewed at the same time, as one child can follow the other or equally be prevented from speaking because of the other. This can change if the child is particularly young or shy and will not speak to CAFCASS under any other circumstances.

If the CAFCASS officer's recommendation is based in any way on what the child has said, then it is important that the process of speaking to the child is done as openly and fairly as possible. However, it is not always the case that children are seen alone in neutral venues. Some schools do not approve of children being interviewed by CAFCASS officers on their premises as they consider that school is meant to be a safe haven for the child and such meetings can disrupt this. It brings a parental dispute into the classroom. Due to time constraints and in cases where a child is not having any contact at all with a parent, children are sometimes interviewed at one parent's home without the chance for a second interview at another parent's home. Some children can refuse to be seen separately.

The circumstances of the child's interview may therefore be grounds for challenging the CAFCASS officer's conclusion. It can also be the case that you may feel the officer has put too much weight, or not enough weight, on a child's view. There may also be a disagreement if a party feels the officer's report is one-sided, for example, against one party, and there may be insufficient balance.

It is not the role of CAFCASS to decide whether domestic violence has taken place, but it may be that the children talk to CAFCASS about things they say they have seen in the parents' relationship. This can feel unfair to the parent accused of bad behaviour, even if all the Officer is doing is reporting what the children have said. A CAFCASS officer should not replace the Court as the decision maker in cases of disputed facts.

This is not an exhaustive list but gives examples of the ways in which an officer's report can be properly criticised.

You may have a personality clash with the officer. However, personal attacks on the CAFCASS officer will not go down well with the Court, so this method of challenging the report should be avoided.

It is also wise not to suggest that the officer and one of the parties are friends (unless you have proof) or that they are biased (again unless you have proof). To question their professional integrity rarely benefits a person's case, particularly with respect to professional independent CAFCASS officers.

THE FINAL HEARING

It will be common for the Court to call the CAFCASS officer to give their evidence at a Final Hearing before anyone else. This is because as a professional witness they would normally need to leave Court as quickly as possible to return to work on other cases.

This, however, may be unhelpful to your case. You may think it is really important that they hear you cross-examine a witness or hear someone else's evidence as this may alter their recommendation. However, there is also a risk that it may entrench their opinion.

You can ask the Court to hear their evidence later and if there is a good reason the Court will normally allow this to happen.

There are also other reports, which CAFCASS can complete within Children Act proceedings, where it thinks it necessary.

SECTION 37 REPORTS

Section 37 Reports are generally outside the scope of this book and when a Section 37 Order is made by the Court you should immediately seek legal advice because it can be the commencement of care proceedings that can result in children being removed into Local Authority care.

If the Court becomes concerned during proceedings about the harm arising from the family breakdown or abuse within the family to which the child or children are being exposed, then it can seek a report under Section 37 of the Children Act.

Where it seems to the Court that it might be appropriate for a Care Order or Supervision Order to be made, then it will direct a Local Authority to undertake an investigation of the child's circumstances and report its findings to the Court. The timescale for completing this report is 8 weeks.

During the investigation, the social worker conducting it will need to consider:

◆ if the Local Authority should consider applying for a Care Order;

◆ if the Local Authority should provide services or assistance for the child and her/his family;

◆ if the Local Authority should take any other action in relation to the child.

The Section 37 Report must cover:

◆ details of the background to the issue;

◆ a history of any Children's Services and/or other agency interventions;

◆ a profile of each child;

◆ a profile of each adult who is party to the proceedings;

◆ the response of the family members to the current circumstances;

◆ a summary of the social worker's assessment;

◆ the social worker's analysis of the Welfare Checklist;

◆ the social worker's comments regarding the 'no order' principle and its relevance to this case;

◆ the social worker's conclusions and recommendations, with detailed reasons.

If the conclusion of the report is to initiate Care Proceedings, then the Local Authority would seek to make an application to the Court as a matter of urgency.

If the conclusion is that the provision of services to the family is required, then the Local Authority would set out a detailed description of those services which would be included within report, together with an indication of the timescales for which the provision of services should be given.

If the conclusion is to take no further action but to review the family circumstances, then the report will need to inform the Court when this review will take place.

RULE 16.4 GUARDIAN

Where the parties are going through court proceedings and it becomes clear to the Court that matters are becoming particularly complicated, then the Court may decide to make the 'child' a party to the proceedings. This does not mean that the child will actually attend court himself. The child will be represented in the proceedings by either a CAFCASS or NYAS officer (see below).

This means that an independent social worker employed by either CAFCASS or NYAS will speak on behalf of the child and make sure that the decisions made about the child are in their best interests. It means that they will become a party to the proceedings and will be allowed to give evidence, cross-examine witnesses and provide reports to the Court.

This situation is becoming more common where the parties find themselves involved in intractable disputes, or where a child or children are refusing to spend time with a parent and the Court needs the assistance of an independent third party to properly understand why this is happening.

This situation is regulated in law by Rule 16.4 of the Family Procedure Rules and this is why it is often referred to as the Rule 16.4 Guardian. They will instruct a Solicitor who specialises in family law to act for your child and represent them in the proceedings. Sometimes the Court may allow older children to instruct their own Solicitor, where their view is different to the view of their Guardian.

The Guardian's role will be to advise the Court on what they think is best for the child, based on their assessment of your case. They will usually meet with the child and the parties to determine the issues. They will want to find out practical things about the child, such as their health and emotional well-being and any special needs they may have. They will also want to know whether the child has suffered any harm (emotional or physical) or has witnessed or been a victim of domestic violence.

They will prepare a report to advise the Court of their analysis and recommendations. In many ways this is very similar to the Section 7 Reports (dealt with earlier, see page 136).

WHO ARE NYAS?

NYAS stands for the National Youth Advocacy Service and it is a UK charity. It can be appointed by the Courts to act as a Rule 16.4 Guardian. It employs professional social workers who can also work with children in a sympathetic and delicate fashion.

SEPARATED PARENTS INFORMATION PROGRAMME (SPIP)

The Court can make a Court Activity Order for parents to attend a Separated Parents Information Programme as part of any private law application. In some cases this can be grandparents or step-parents. This is a short course, often run in one or two sessions, designed to help inform parents about the challenges in caring for a child post separation and the effects on children of an on-going parental dispute. The needs of the child are central to the programme.

The aim of the programme is to assist parents to find better ways to communicate with one another without the need for conflict or disharmony. It reminds them that the child must be their priority and of the emotional harm that the child will suffer as a result of any conflict caused by parental separation.

The SPIP is particularly helpful because it encourages both parents to view things from the child's perspective, to listen and reflect, and to communicate with one another and to manage conflict more effectively.

You will not be expected to attend the course at the same venue and time as the other parent. However, there will be other parents on the course and you will have the opportunity for group discussions. This will enable you to speak openly about your situation. It is mandatory to participate if the Court has made an Order to attend.

Most parents that go on the course find it both helpful and beneficial.

At the end of the programme you will be provided with a Certificate and you may need to show this to the Court to confirm attendance.

The Court will provide you with the details of the service providers for your area when it makes such an Order.

13

Experts' Reports

TYPES OF EXPERT

There are occasions when the Court can be asked to consider the
need for any expert evidence. This is essentially evidence from a
professional who is not a CAFCASS officer, Guardian or social
worker.

You may be asked to produce evidence from your GP or any
treating doctor if it is alleged that you have a relevant medical
condition such as depression or a physical condition that affects
your ability to care for the child. You can also ask for the other
side to produce this information about themselves. There is usually
a charge for this and the GP involved will need to be given some
time to write any report. It is very rare for a GP to be called to give
evidence at a trial.

It is also possible to ask for specific doctors or other experts to write
reports just for the purpose of court proceedings. This can include
but is not limited to psychiatric or psychological assessments of a
parent or child and also specialist risk assessments.

Finally, there are specialist tests that you can ask to be carried
out. The Court can, for example, order DNA testing to establish

paternity. This is most likely to be used to establish whether a party to the proceedings is a father to the child. Hair-strand tests can also be ordered to check for drug and alcohol misuse.

Scientific testing

The science behind hair-strand tests is complicated but, in essence, whenever you ingest a substance such as drugs or alcohol, your body breaks it down. When the substance has been used up, byproducts (or 'metabolites') remain in the body. They can be identified in your hair. Given that our hair grows at a slow but steady rate, it is usually possible for a hair-strand testing company to divide any hair sample into sections, showing a month at a time. The test identifies the levels of the byproducts in the body. It can be possible for the level of the metabolites to be so low that it does not meet the necessary level to register as a positive test. This might be, for example, if the drug was only used once, or contact to the drug was limited; for example, passively inhaling cannabis smoke by virtue of sitting next to someone using it on one occasion is unlikely to register as a positive result.

On the other hand, it may not be possible to say whether a positive result means that a drug was actually taken. It may show what can be called a 'positive association' with the drug instead. That could be the outcome where the levels are consistent with either use of cannabis or being in repeated contact with others using it.

It is not always possible for a testing company to be able to say exactly how much alcohol was drunk or how much of a drug was taken. Any hair-strand analysis will therefore need to come with a report explaining what the results say.

Head or body hair is suitable for analysis, with head hair being the preferred type. When a sample is given, the person having the test is asked to declare any tablets they are taking, and whether they have used products on their hair. This is because it can affect the results.

If you are asked to take one of these tests, it is often better to be open with the Court at the outset as to what you expect it to show.

If the test is ordered and you do not cooperate with it; for example, by cutting your hair very short, bleaching it or using other chemicals, the other side can ask the Court to assume from this that the test would have been positive. It can be sensible if you are seeking the hair-strand test to ask the Court at the time of the Order being made to explain to the person giving the sample the consequences of not complying.

In terms of DNA testing, this will obviously require DNA from the child and potential father. The test can be more accurate if DNA is also taken from the mother, although that is not absolutely essential. The Courts are required to use companies from an approved list. There will be a charge for DNA testing and this will depend on the number of children/adults to be tested and how quickly the results are needed. The Court will not order DNA tests as a matter of routine. You will need to explain why you are concerned about paternity. The Court would expect parents to cooperate with any testing ordered and may draw inferences from any failure to cooperate.

When DNA testing is ordered from older children, careful thought has to be given to what explanation should be given to the child as to why the test is being done so as to minimise any disruption or worry to the child. The collecting of the DNA itself is not invasive – it is usually taken by a swab and is unlikely to be painful.

Other expert assessments

The majority of applications for a Child Arrangements Order will proceed with evidence from either CAFCASS or Social Services and any medical issues can often be resolved by a letter from a GP or consultant.

There can, however, be times when a case is more complicated than this; perhaps a medical condition is more significant or unusual so that a specific report is needed from an expert in that field, or the case has become very entrenched so that a psychologist could be of use in helping the Court understand what is going on.

Experts have a particularly important status in family law. That is not to say that the Court will always follow what they say, but they have been chosen to provide evidence to the Court in an area that is beyond the understanding of the 'usual' professionals and parties involved in a case.

The main difference between instructing an independent expert and inviting, for example, a parent's GP to write a letter is that an independent expert is under specific duties to help the Court and can be called to court to give evidence and answer questions. That is not usually the case when the doctor concerned is the treating doctor.

These are some examples of the sort of circumstances in which the Court can consider instructing an expert. Each case does depend on its own facts though, so do not think you cannot ask for an expert simply because your case does not match anything on this list:

- The parents of a child disagree over whether the child should remain educated at home by the mother, or attend mainstream school. Court proceedings have been brought by the father asking that the child should attend the local primary school. The mother states that the child has anxiety and some learning needs that are best dealt with at home. The Court may be helped by a report from an educational psychologist who can assess the child and advise the Court about his/her learning needs.

- A father has been having contact with his son at a contact centre for some time. There is now no safeguarding reason why the father cannot take the child out of the contact centre for contact but every time this is attempted, the child becomes very distressed. There is some suggestion that the child is being investigated for autism, meaning that changes in routine are very stressful. The Court may consider ordering a report from a child psychologist to look at the child's needs and offer advice to assist those managing contact to help the child move on.

- A parent has been found to have been violent and abusive in a relationship. They now seek contact with their child and say that they have changed. A psychological assessment can be used to assess the risk they now pose.

- A child lives with her mother and there is a history in the case of contact with her father starting and then breaking down. The father says this is because her mother is influencing the child. The mother says this is because the father is not committed to contact and the child is upset about going. The case has been going on for a very long time and the issues have not been resolved with help from CAFCASS. A psychological assessment of the family can help to identity what the issues are.

It is also possible to order specific risk assessments to cover other types of concern. Where sexual abuse is an issue, for example, there are experts within this field who can assess people's risk of offending. The key to assessments such as these is that the Court must consider them 'necessary' and the Court must have already decided on the factual background to the case (more about this later).

It should also be said that instructing experts to prepare a report is often a sign that your case is potentially very complicated and so you should really give consideration to seeking legal advice where you can. This book is intended to provide you with some background information but it is not intended to be a replacement for legal advice.

INSTRUCTING AN EXPERT TO WRITE A REPORT

Experts in family cases are usually instructed jointly. This means both or all parties are involved in the instruction. You cannot cause a child to be medically examined for court proceedings without the authority of the Court. This is made clear in Section 13 of the Children and Families Act 2014.

Simply taking your child to an expert to be examined to get a report to support your case, without permission from the Court and without allowing the other parties to also ask questions of the expert, is not allowed. If you choose to do this, you are likely to be criticised and you will not be allowed to rely upon the evidence in that report.

Similarly, if you try to get an expert report, even without causing your child to be examined without the permission of the Court, you will not be allowed to rely on the report.

This is not the same as taking a child to the doctor because he or she is unwell and that doctor, for example, reporting in the medical notes that the child has expressed anxiety about a particular issue. That medical note would be taken as part of medical treatment for the child and will not be given the status of an 'expert' examination.

Before coming to court, you should identify in advance not only the type of expert you are going to need and, specifically, which expert you want to instruct. The Court will need to know this and will also need a copy of their CV and other details to be able to make an informed decision. It is not unusual for a party seeking an expert to offer the Court a choice of more than one expert.

You will also need to get details of how much that expert will charge and how long it will take to prepare their report. If a Final Hearing date has been set in your case, you will need to know if the expert you have in mind is available to attend that hearing to give evidence. If a Final Hearing date has not been set, then it would still be helpful to know when they are available or dates to avoid in case the Court wants to set a Final Hearing date.

When you ask for the costs of the report, you need to get a total figure and to clarify whether or not it includes VAT. You will also need the expert's hourly rate.

You will need to make a paper application for the expert to be instructed. This is done on Form C2.

When a joint expert is instructed, one party needs to take the lead. They are often called the 'lead instruction' and are responsible for contacting the expert to arrange appointments and sending agreed papers to them. This can be a complicated job. If you are against a party who is represented, then it is likely to be suggested that this is to be done by the Solicitor. It does not give any party the right to try to influence the expert in their conclusions, it is purely administrative.

IN WHAT CIRCUMSTANCES WILL THE COURT ORDER AN EXPERT?

The short answer is that the Court will order an expert only when it is necessary to resolve the proceedings justly. This is clear from both Part 25 of the Family Procedure Rules 2010 and Section 13 of the Children and Families Act 2014. The use of the word 'necessary' is taken to mean that there has to be a need for the evidence.

Therefore, you should be prepared to justify any application you make for an expert. Where the expert report you propose involves an examination of the child, the Court will need to give permission and this permission needs to be written into the Order.

WHO WILL PAY FOR THE EXPERT?

Experts' reports can be costly (anything from a few hundred to thousands of pounds) but where they are necessary, the Court will need to decide how those costs are paid. There are a number of scenarios.

Cases in which both parents are not legally represented

In this case, where there is no public funding, the Court is likely to require the parties to pay for the report and will make a decision as to how the costs should be divided.

Cases in which one parent is legally represented

In this case, depending on the type of report ordered, the costs of the report can be paid in part by the legally aided parent's public funding, although it would be very unusual for this to be anything other than 50 per cent of the costs. The balance will have to be made up by the other party.

Cases with a Guardian or a Solicitor for the Child

When a child is appointed as a party to proceedings, he or she will be eligible for Legal Aid. If the Court orders the parties to share the costs of a report equally, this means that the number of parties to divide the costs among becomes three, not two. Therefore, the share you pay as a person representing themselves becomes a third and not a half.

It should be pointed out, however, that the share is divided between the number of Legal Aid certificates and not the number of children. If you have more than one child represented by a Guardian, they still only count as one party for the purpose of funding a report.

Where the report is not asked for by the parents, but asked for by the Guardian as a single (and not a joint) expert, it is possible for the Legal Aid Agency to be asked to pay for it in total out of the child's Legal Aid certificate. This is not a decision the Court can direct or easily enforce and it is unlikely to be done except in exceptional circumstances.

Do not assume, however, that expert reports will automatically be funded. Be prepared to attend court with evidence as to your means if you intend to argue that you cannot afford to pay for a report, because this will save time and assist the Court in making the right Order.

There are some very rare circumstances where the Court can be asked to cover some of the legal costs.

DISAGREEING WITH THE EXPERT REPORT

The Court has ordered an expert report to be prepared and I disagree. Do I have to take part?

If an expert is ordered to prepare a report, it will be because the Judge was persuaded it was necessary. The Judge has the power to order an expert to report without the consent of all of the parties. If a report is ordered without your consent you firstly need to consider whether you have grounds of appeal.

As you will see later in this book, the decision to order an expert report is a case management decision. Appeals against these decisions are not to be entered into lightly and so you really should think carefully before doing so. You may want to consider legal advice.

If the decision to order an expert is not appealed, it stands. If you don't comply with it, the Court can be invited by the other side to 'draw inferences' from that non-compliance. The effects of this can be serious. If, for example, you are ordered to take part in a psychological assessment because there is an issue around whether you pose a risk because of past domestic abuse and you don't comply, the Court can be asked to infer from your non-compliance that you still pose a risk.

If a report has been ordered and this Order is not set aside, then you should comply with it. If you then disagree with the conclusions of the report once it is written, you will have the chance to challenge it at a Final Hearing.

It is important to remember that you could also be liable for any costs incurred by the expert for any missed appointments if you are found to have deliberately not attended.

Similar points apply to hair-strand and DNA tests. If you refuse to cooperate with these, the Court can be asked to infer that, again, you wish to hide drug use or are avoiding clarifying the issue of paternity. The Court is less likely to order a hair-strand or DNA test if you do not agree but it may be written on the Court Order that you were offered the chance to do such a test but declined and therefore inferences may be drawn.

Again, if an Order is made for such testing, you should comply with it (if it is not appealed or set aside) or risk inferences and costs.

14

Witness Statements in Family Proceedings

Prior to a Finding of Fact Hearing or a contested Final Hearing it will be necessary for you (and the other party) to set out in writing everything you want to say to the Court (this is called evidence) in a document that is called a witness statement. This is an extremely important document and great care must be taken in drafting it. An example of a witness statement is set out below.

A witness statement is your opportunity to explain to the Court and the other parties in writing your views, concerns and proposals.

In many ways it is as if you are writing a letter to the Court setting out relevant history with regard to the relationship with the parent and child, any difficulties and then, where appropriate, your proposals for the future.

It is a formal document and it is crucial that the contents of the statement are true.

At the end of the witness statement you will have to make a declaration to the Court that the witness statement is 'true to the best of your knowledge and belief'.

This is not a promise to the other party but to the Court. The Court can apply sanctions should you breach this promise. Courts take this very seriously and it may harm your case if you are shown to have included things that are false.

When considering any application, the Court will read the witness statements of the parties. The other side and the Court are likely to have questions about the contents of the statement. This may be to clarify something or to challenge the contents.

THE LEGAL BIT

It is extremely important that when you attend either a Finding of Fact Hearing or a Final Hearing you know what the other party is going to say and they know what you are saying. It is not fair to turn up at court and ambush the other party or be ambushed by the other side. Hearing an allegation or a statement for the first time at court does not give you an opportunity to think about what they are saying and work out your response. For this reason the Court will normally order that witness statements are prepared by all witnesses who propose to give evidence and that these statements are exchanged prior to the hearing. The normal order is:

'the mother and father file and serve all the evidence which they wish to rely on by witness statement by 2pm on xx/xx/ xxxx'

'Filing' means submitting the witness statement to the Court. 'Serving' means sending the statement to the other parties in proceedings. This can be done by first class post or delivered by hand to the Court. It is advisable to send all documents by recorded delivery so that you have proof that you have sent them on time.

While this has a cost to it, it will also give you proof that you have complied with the Court Order and prevent any other party saying that they have not received it, which can sometimes be suggested. You should of course keep a copy for yourself.

In Finding of Fact Hearings, or where it is necessary for one party to respond to allegations being made by the other party, it is quite common for the Court to order that one party prepares their witness statement first and then the other party will normally have about two weeks to consider that statement and to submit their statement in response. For example:

'(1) the father do file and serve all the evidence which he wishes to rely on by witness statement by 2pm on xx/xx/xxxx'

'(2) the mother do file and serve all the evidence which she wishes to rely on by witness statement by 2pm on xx/xx/xxxx [two weeks later]'

It is not uncommon in some cases for each party to file more than one witness statement during the proceedings, as further issues or situations arise.

HOW TO DRAFT A WITNESS STATEMENT AND WHAT TO INCLUDE

The Format of the Statement
The statement must be in writing. It should be typed in double-line spacing and be printed on white A4 paper.

This makes the statement much easier to read and photocopy. This is very important. Most of us have terrible handwriting and it is much quicker and easier to read a typed document. The last thing

you want to do is to annoy the Court even before you open your
mouth by submitting a handwritten statement, which is difficult and
time-consuming to read.

Each page should be numbered. The paragraphs must also be
numbered. This is important as it allows the Court and the parties
to turn to the right page and right part of the statement easily and
quickly. Keep it concise, keep it simple and keep it accurate.

In the top *right*-hand side of each page, you should add the
following:

> *Filed on behalf of [add in your name]*

> *Exhibits [   ]*

> *Dated: XX.XX.XX [the date you are signing and sending the
> statement to the Court]*

> Case Number: [   ] (This number can be found on
> the application form that has been issued by the Court. It is
> usually a 9–11 combination of letters and numbers. This is a
> unique number, which identifies your case to the Court.)

On the *left*-hand side of the document you need to state the name
of the Court. This is where the application is being heard. For
example:

> In the Family Court sitting at [Windsor].

In most cases this is then followed by:

In the matter of the Children Act 1989

And in the matter of [the child's name and date of birth]

In the centre of the document you need to include the names of the parties and their status in the case. You state the applicant's name first and this is followed by the name of each respondent (if there are more than one).

For example:

ANNA SMITH

<u>Applicant</u>

and

DARREN SMITH

<u>Respondent</u>

If there is more than one respondent (for example, if a grandparent has become a party to the case), it will read as follows:

ANNA SMITH

<u>Applicant</u>

and

DARREN SMITH

<u>1st Respondent</u>

and

MOIRA AND PETER SMITH

2nd and 3rd Respondents

In either case it will be followed by a heading of:

WITNESS STATEMENT OF [add in your name]

The first paragraph of your witness statement will tell the Court who you are and where you live. For example:

I, Darren Smith, of 21 Main Street, Bordesley Green, Birmingham, B67 4DN, will say as follows:

If you do not wish to tell the other parties where you live you can state:

I, Darren Smith, of confidential address, will say as follows:

The first paragraph should set the scene for the Court and explain who you are and why you are making a statement. Keep it short and to the point. For example:

(1) I am the father of Megan Smith (DOB 04.05.06) and Megan lives with me. I am making this statement in response to an application by Anna Smith, Megan's mother, for a Child Arrangements Order in which she wishes to see Megan every fortnight from Friday night to Sunday evening.

You will then go on to explain what your views are on the application within the rest of the statement. This should be where possible in a chronological order and kept simple. The witness statement should be written in the first person: 'I think' and 'told me'.

Try to keep the information in the statement fair and balanced. Remind yourself of this key point: if I was reading this statement and knew nothing about the parties and the case, does it make sense and does it seem fair?

Keep each paragraph to a reasonable length. In other words, anything over about 10 lines is pushing it because it becomes hard work to read. If there are different parts to the application, e.g. an application for a Child Arrangements Order for increased time with the child and also an application for the child to be known by a different name, you may want to use headings for each separate part of the statement.

For example:

Megan's time with her mother

Megan's surname

This will assist the Court when reading your application to know which part of the application you are dealing with and will mean the reader does not have to jump around your statement trying to find the points you are making on each issue.

What are exhibits?

Exhibits are usually written documents that you wish to rely on and wish to show to the Court. For example, they might be letters, emails, immigration paperwork, GP notes, school reports, copies of text messages (you will need to copy them out into a document), Facebook pages, reports from domestic violence work, probation reports, etc.

You must include any document that is relevant to your case and which you intend to talk about at the hearing. If you are referring to records or Police statements in your witness statement then make it clear that this is where the evidence is coming from and attach that document as an exhibit.

This does not mean you should include every document you possess! This might be thorough but having to wade through a 100-page witness statement and exhibits that are not relevant will annoy the Court. If you turn up to a hearing and say that you have left a relevant document at home, the Court is unlikely to stop the hearing to allow you to get it so spend some time thinking about what you want to exhibit well in advance.

Relevant exhibits may be:

- medical records

- accident and emergency records

- Police callout logs or statements

- letter from the school or school reports

- OFSTED reports

◆ flight details concerning a holiday

◆ employment contract

◆ telephone records

◆ dental records

◆ tenancy agreement

◆ letters or copies of text messages

Where you do not have copies of these records, such as Police call-out records or GP or hospital records, then you can ask the Court to make an Order for these records to be obtained from either the Police or the GP/hospital. The Court should be able to help you with the wording of any such Order and you will also need to be clear as to the cost of obtaining the records and who will be paying that cost. You will also want to be clear as to whether you are sending a copy of the Order asking for the information to the Police or GP/hospital or whether the other party will be sending it. It is not enough for you to tell the Court that it can check what you are saying with the Police or with a third party – the responsibility is on you to obtain the information.

Exhibits can also be photographs. It is worth ensuring that the photographs are of good quality and in colour, if possible. This is because there is nothing worse than trying to show the Court a detail in a photograph to find that it cannot properly be seen because it has been badly printed or photocopied. You may also wish to bring spare copies to court.

You may also have relevant audio or video evidence that you wish to exhibit. If the audio or video is very long and includes irrelevant sections you may wish to edit it down. However, be careful not to edit out relevant sections or context. You do not want the other party to suggest that you have edited the evidence to show them in a bad light or you in a good light, when the full clip shows a different story. You should also tell the Court and the parties in your witness statement by what and how you have edited it. If you do want to exhibit audio or video you will need to provide copies that can be played by the Court and the other side, e.g. copied on to a CD or DVD. Again, you will need to disclose this material prior to the Final Hearing. Do not presume that the Court has the best facility to actually hear or watch such material and you will need to check with the Court in advance the best way for the material to be considered.

Exhibits should be seen as an extension to your statement. They must be true to the best of your knowledge and belief. You will need to prepare a sheet that introduces each exhibit and includes a Statement of Truth.

An example exhibit sheet has been prepared.

Each exhibit needs to have a reference number. If your name is Anna Smith, your first exhibit will be referenced AS1, your second AS2, your third AS3 and so on.

At the end of your witness statement, you must add a Statement of Truth. This should read:

'I believe that the facts stated in this Witness Statement are true.'

Signed.....................................

Date.....................................

As explained above, the Court will not be pleased if you confirm that the statement is true but you are later shown to have included something that is false. This is contempt of court. It also undermines your credibility – in other words the Court may not believe what you say about other things. Remember you will be questioned on the content of the statement under oath.

If this all seems pedantic, it is! However, it will ensure that your statement creates the right impression and gets your case off to a good start.

So what else needs to go in the witness statement?
These are basic requirements for a witness statement. There are, however, some other tips which should assist your case.

The purpose of the witness statement is to set out your story in full but concise detail. It should make it clear to the Court that you are child focused, reasonable and that the welfare of your child is your paramount consideration.

For Finding of Fact Hearings you will need to stress the following:

◆ the basis of your relationship with the other party. How long you have known them; if there was a relationship, what is the start date and what is the end date;

- any children arising from the relationship, with their names and dates of birth. This would usually be the child or children to whom the application relates;

- any other children who may be relevant. For example, step-children whom you may see regularly and/or anyone who may see the relevant child/children regularly;

- who has been the primary carer of the relevant child/ren and what involvement the other party has had in their upbringing. Try to be as fair and as objective as possible in this analysis;

- each and every element of physical/emotional abuse or neglect. Always start with the first incident and set out what happened in as much detail as possible. For each incident where possible write about one clear and detailed paragraph;

- in a chronological fashion set out the next incident and so on;

- you should also explain for each incident whether it was witnessed by any person. If not, whom you told about it and when. Do you have any additional evidence to prove that the incident took place? Are there photographs? If so, attach as exhibits. Did you go to the Police or to the GP? If not, why not? You will probably be asked these types of questions at the Final Hearing in an attempt to dispute your version of events so it is best, if at all possible, to deal with such questions directly in your witness statement;

- as many of these incidents will have happened some time ago, it is an idea to check what you may have written in any diaries or indeed in any Police logs that were taken at the time. It is very important to ensure that you tell the truth and that all statements (including perhaps previous Police statements) are accurate.

For Final Hearings you should stress the following:

◈ the basis of your relationship with the other party. How long you have known them; if there was a relationship when is the start date and when is the end date;

◈ any children arising from the relationship, with their names and dates of birth. This would usually be the child or children to whom the application relates;

◈ any other children who may be relevant, such as step-children whom you may see regularly and/or who may see the relevant child/children regularly;

◈ who has been the primary carer of the relevant child/ren and what involvement has the other party had in their upbringing. Try to be as fair and as objective as possible in this analysis.

◈ any safeguarding issues – this will include any relevant intervention from the Police or Children's Services. If there are any drink, drug or abuse/violence issues then these should be set out in a chronological fashion;

◈ what efforts have been made between the two of you to avoid this matter coming to court;

◈ what your view is of the application and any proposals you would make;

◈ the effect, if any, on the child/ren of the application and the possible outcomes;

◈ it is also very helpful and assists the Court if you give consideration to the Welfare Checklist in your statement. Go through the Welfare Checklist in your statement, using each element of the checklist, perhaps as headings. Set out paragraph by paragraph how the checklist applies to your child/ren and this application.

◆ For example:

  ◆ the ascertainable wishes and feelings of the child concerned (considered in the light of his age and understanding):

  'My child [name] who is twelve years of age has made it perfectly clear to me that while he wants to spend time with his mother, he wants to live with me. He has also made this clear to the CAFCASS officer at paragraph 6.2 of her report dated xx/xx/xxxx where it is recorded that he states 'I want to live with Dad.'

  ◆ his physical, emotional and educational needs:

  'While there are no specific physical or emotional needs relevant to this application, should [name] move and live with his mother, then this will mean that he needs to change school. As he is approaching his exams and is doing very well at school it would not be appropriate to move him. This is particularly the position as the school he goes to at present is rated by Ofsted as being outstanding (see exhibit JJ1) and the school which mother proposes to move him to is only rated as being good (see exhibit JJ2).'

  ◆ the likely effect on him of any change in his circumstances:

  'My child [name] has been living with me since birth. He is now twelve years old. It would be a significant change in circumstances if he was to move and live with the other parent in a new house and new part of town.'

◆ his age, sex, background and any characteristics of his which the Court considers relevant:

'My child is three years old and is delayed in her speech and language. She began attending a nursery two months ago and has regular appointments with a speech and language therapist. She is making progress through these measures. Any change would disrupt this progress.'

◆ any harm which he has suffered or is at risk of suffering:

'My son has experienced physical harm as set out above while in his mother's care. She does not accept that she did this and there is a risk that without either suitable supervision or him living with me, this will continue. She has not undertaken any behaviour management/parenting classes which might lessen the risk of there being more harm.'

◆ how capable each of his parents, and any other person in relation to whom the Court considers the question to be relevant, are of meeting his needs:

'It is accepted that both parents can care equally well for the child.'

◆ the range of powers available to the Court under this Act in the proceedings in question:

'I would seek the Court to make a Child Arrangements Order for [name] to live with me and to see the other party once a week.'

To reiterate, the Welfare Checklist is vital in family proceedings and in most cases is the test that the Court must consider when making final decisions. If you can draw to the Court's attention in your witness statement how the checklist can be applied to the facts of your specific case, such as in the examples above, this should be very helpful.

You may struggle to apply each element in the checklist but do not worry if this happens. Not every element of the checklist will apply to every case. But where it does apply ensure that you have made reference to that element of the checklist in your witness statement.

Once you have drafted your witness statement it is often a good idea to leave it for a short period of time (perhaps overnight) and then re-read it. Check afresh whether it says what you want it to say. If someone read it who had never met you before (the Court perhaps) does it make sense? Are there any gaps in the evidence or mistakes?

Make any changes as necessary and then do a spell check.

Letters in support

It should also be noted that references or letters of support from friends and family often carry little weight in court and should, in most cases, be avoided. This is because most people can find friends or family members who will happily write letters in support. The Court does not seek to invite a popularity contest. It is only interested in statements from those people who actually have something relevant to add to the proceeding, such as a friend or family member willing to offer support by way of childcare or an extra pair of hands.

Other witnesses

Where friends or family members have witnessed domestic violence or domestic abuse, which is relevant to a finding being sought in a Finding of Fact Hearing, then they should prepare witness statements.

Their statements must follow the same court format and headings.

It will also be necessary for them to sign a Statement of Truth at the end of the statement. You should advise them that their statement must be true to the best of their knowledge and belief, that the statement will be used in court proceedings and read by the Court. You should also point out to them that they may be called to give evidence and can of course be cross-examined as to the facts in the case, including what they have written in their witness statement. It is thus not as simple as writing a statement and thinking that is the end of it.

The statement should also set out the following:

- how they know the parties;

- their relationship to you;

- what they witnessed. It is vitally important that if you do help them to draft this witness statement you use their language rather than your own. It is their statement and it must be genuine. Do not cut and paste the relevant paragraph from your witness statement and simply insert it in their statement;

- their statement should be set out chronologically and be both concise and balanced;

- if their statement is going to have any weight with the Court it must be genuine and from them, not you.

SIMPLE RULES FOR WRITING WITNESS STATEMENTS

Keep it simple, clear, concise and child focused.

Write the way you talk, naturally.

Use short words, short sentences and never more than 10 lines to a paragraph.

There is never any reason for your witness statement to be any more than 8 pages.

Does it convey you in your best light and does it make it clear what you are asking the Court to do?

Never send it on the day you write it. Read it aloud the next morning and if necessary make any amendments.

Once it is finished read it three times before you approve it.

If you are happy with your witness statement and the exhibits then sign the witness statement and take four copies. Send or deliver two copies to the Court and send a copy to the other side. Keep a copy for yourself.

15

The Final Hearing

PRIOR TO ATTENDING COURT

The evening before the court hearing you should re-read all the papers in the case. In particular re-read your witness statement, the other party's witness statement and also the CAFCASS report, if there is one.

What do I actually want from the Court?

Be clear in your mind what your position is on all the issues in dispute. The Court will want to know what you have to say about all of the issues.

If you are calling any witnesses to support your case at the Final Hearing, you should inform them well in advance of your intention to do so as they may have commitments that they will have to re-arrange. You should also remind them closer to the date of the time and location of the court hearing and also advise them to re-read their witness statement.

Make sure you take all your papers to court. It will help you if you have all of the relevant documentation within a ring binder as this will allow you to turn to each page easily and quietly. You do not want to be rummaging nosily through a carrier bag stuffed with papers to keep up with what the Judge and the other parties are looking at. Also bring a notebook and a pen.

Court bundle

The Court will expect an agreed bundle of documents to be prepared between the parties, which will then be placed before the Court. A bundle simply means a folder of documents, which has an index and includes page numbers. Ideally all parties have the same bundle, which allows all parties and the Court to easily turn to the correct page. The responsibility for preparing the bundle usually falls on the Applicant. However, if one party is legally represented, the responsibility falls upon them. The bundle should be in a ring binder, which is large and secure enough for the pages to be easily turned. There should be a section for the Application and Court Orders, a section for the witness statement/any other documentation relied upon by the Applicant and a section for the witness statement/ any other documentation relied upon by the Respondent(s). There may also need to be sections for expert evidence, such as CAFCASS or Local Authority Reports, and further sections for other documentation such as medical records/Police records. However, what is most important is that the documents are all given a page number and are in chronological order. There should be an index at the start of the bundle that sets out what each document is and the page numbers for that document. This is essentially a Contents page. If the responsibility is with you to file a copy of the bundle with the Court, this will usually need to be done within five working days of the hearing – but it is wise to ask the Court to confirm the date by which it should be filed with them. You should send a copy of the index to the other party to allow them to check the documents within it. You should, of course, ensure that the court bundle is accurate and contains all of the documents that have been circulated during proceedings.

ARRIVAL AT COURT

The Court will have indicated the time and date for the Final Hearing. You will have a section on the previous Court Order or Notice of Hearing document from the Court, which sets out these details. It usually also states that the parties are to attend court either 30 or 60 minutes prior to the hearing to attempt to reduce the issues between the parties. Make sure you leave plenty of time to get to court as you do not want to arrive late and stressed. Many Courts will start a case on time whether you are there or not and can make Court Orders in your absence.

Signing in

On arrival at the court building you will need to locate the Court Usher and sign in to check that you are at the right court. Your case will not usually be listed by name but by the case number (the number on the court papers).

You should tell the Court Usher where you are going to sit to wait and also find out if the other party has arrived and whether Counsel or a Solicitor represents them. If CAFCASS are instructed to attend court then you may also wish to ask whether they have arrived yet.

It is very important to sign in with the Court Usher as it can happen that a case will get called into court and if you are not paying attention or the usher does not know that you have arrived the Court may complete the case in your absence.

What if your case is not listed?

This can happen and on the rare occasion it *does* happen. The Court Office does occasionally make mistakes and sometimes lists hearings for the wrong time or date. Sometimes the case will get adjourned and the Court will forget to tell the parties. If it is not listed show a copy of your Notice of Hearing or last Court Order to the Court Usher and they will try to resolve the issue for you. Whatever you do, do not simply go home without the issue having been resolved there and then. If it has been adjourned or there has been an error, try to resolve with the court staff what the problem is and the rearranged date (where possible).

NEGOTIATION

It is very common for cases to be resolved outside of court on the day of the Final Hearing. Often the very fact that a case has now reached the Final Hearing or perhaps the prospect of giving evidence in court becomes more real and stressful or the preference to make the final decision rather than have it adjudicated on by a third person is sufficient for the parties to attempt to reach an amicable agreement to the dispute at the door of the Court. A chat with your opponent or their lawyer may be able to resolve the matter without either party giving any evidence. Indeed, matters may well have improved since the commencement of court proceedings. If agreement can be reached it is still appropriate to go before the Court to have the agreement recorded and approved by way of a Court Order. It is always a sensible idea to take notes of any discussions that you have with either the other party or their lawyer just to ensure that you have it clear in your mind what you are agreeing to. Do not allow them to simply bounce you into a settlement if you are not happy with it. However, it is often better to reach agreement where you can do so. The Court will give you a copy of the Court Order and it is usually sensible to ask for a copy of this document at court so that you can read and check it, where possible.

WHO CAN I BRING TO COURT WITH ME?

Firstly, it is never a good idea to bring children with you. You cannot take them into court. It is not as if they can sit at the back of court while you have a row with your ex-partner over whether he is a good parent or not. Equally, the Court itself does not have any childcare facilities and most Judges will be extremely critical of you for bringing the child and it will simply delay matters.

You should always arrange childcare from about an hour before the start of the hearing to ensure that you get to court on time and also until the end of the court day, which is usually 4.30 p.m. This will often mean ensuring that someone else can pick the children up from school or nursery (see below).

Friends and family cannot come into the actual courtroom with you. Children cases are usually heard in private and for this reason you cannot bring other people into the courtroom without the permission of the other party and, more importantly, the Judge. It is extremely rare that the Judge will allow other people to sit in and just watch what is going on in the proceedings. Friends and family can wait in the waiting area with you but you should always remind them to avoid saying anything threatening or inappropriate to the other side. These things invariably get back to the Court and can never help in resolving the case amicably or in your favour.

COURT TIME

The Court usually lists hearings to be heard at 10 a.m or 2 p.m. The problem, however, is that the Court frequently lists lots of cases at the same time. The reason for this is that court time is a precious commodity and this listing ensures that if one case is not ready, another can take its place and little court time is wasted. So you may arrive at court for a hearing that has been allocated 30 minutes of court time at 10 a.m., but you may find that the Court has also listed another ten cases at the same time. You can sometimes use this time to speak with the CAFCASS officer or negotiate, where possible, with the other party. Otherwise it is simply time spent waiting to get into court.

The clerk or legal advisor will normally come to ask whether you are ready to go into court and you should make sure that you speak to them as soon as you are ready so that you can get into court as soon as it becomes free. So on any day when you have a court hearing it is very sensible to ensure that you have childcare and that you have prepared on the basis that you will be at court all day rather than for just the short time as suggested in the listing. It is also a good idea to take with you a packed lunch. As a result of government cuts few courts these days have canteens or even coffee machines. You want to be able to focus on your case and not be worried about childcare arrangements or distracted by how hungry you are!

GOING INTO COURT

Whenever you either go into or leave court you should bow or nod to the court shield, which is normally placed behind the head of the Judge or Magistrates. In addition, everyone in court needs to stand when either the Judge or the Magistrates enter or leave court.

Normally the legal advisor or usher will remind you to do this. You sit down a moment after they sit down. When your case is being heard before a District Judge or Magistrates you can address (speak to) the Court sitting down. If your case is heard before a Circuit Judge then you will need to address the Court standing up.

16

Overview of a Final Hearing

The Judge or Magistrates will have read the court papers (the bundle) prior to the hearing. The Court will often ask for a short opening statement from both parties.

If the CAFCASS officer has been called to give evidence then they will also come into court with the Applicant and the Respondent. They will usually give their evidence first and both the Applicant and the Respondent will be able to cross-examine them as to their evidence. The Judge or Magistrates may also wish to ask their own questions.

The Judge or Magistrates will then hear evidence from the Applicant and then the Respondent will be allowed to cross-examine the Applicant. The Applicant will then call any additional witnesses that they have and they too will be cross-examined by the Respondent. Once the Applicant and their witnesses have all given their evidence then it is the Respondent's turn to call their evidence and they will be cross-examined by the Applicant. The Respondent will call any of their witnesses and they too can be cross-examined by the Applicant. Once the Court has heard all of the evidence then the Respondent is able to make final submissions to the Court and then the Applicant can make their final submissions to the Court. The Court will be able to ask questions at any time.

AN OPENING STATEMENT

If you are the Applicant (the person who has issued the proceedings) at the start of the case you should set out what the case is about and what the Court is being asked to help with. By way of example:

> *'I am Mr George the Applicant and this is Miss Mildred the Respondent. This case is about our daughter Amy, who is 6 years old. Miss Mildred refuses to let me see my daughter and hence this application, which I made for a Child Arrangements Order on 20 November xxxx. I last saw Amy on 14 February xxxx. I would like the Court to order that I see Amy every other weekend from 4pm on a Friday until 6pm on a Sunday. I would also like all holidays to be shared equally.'*

This type of opening statement to the Court is clear and precise. It is always better than a long-winded history of the relationship, which actually tells the Court nothing of any use. The Court may then ask the other party what they consider to be in dispute and they may either agree with what has been said or state something like this:

> *'I agree with everything that he says, but he didn't see Amy on 14 February xxxx. He has not seen her for two years. I think he should see her but supervised in a contact centre and only once a month. I also think it's too early to consider half of all holidays.'*

The Court can then hear evidence and come to a decision.

EVIDENCE

The starting point for evidence at a Final Hearing is the witness statements, which you will have prepared within the proceedings. At the Final Hearing both parties will have an opportunity to challenge the other as to the content of their witness statement or anything else that is relevant to the issues being considered by the Court.

EVIDENCE IN CHIEF

The aim of evidence in chief (also called examination in chief) is to obtain from your witness anything relevant that is not clear from their witness statement, has happened since they have written their witness statement or to seek further clarity on something that has happened. It is also used in family cases where someone is perhaps nervous and by asking them some simple questions it allows them to relax and familiarise themselves with the surroundings. One rule with regard to evidence in chief is that you must not lead your witness. This basically means that the answer to your question should not be in the question. An example of this is to say: 'The sky is blue, isn't it?' The answer to the question, i.e. the sky is blue, has already been said. The evidence needs to come from them and not from you. The golden rule to avoid this problem is to ask questions starting with the words, 'How', 'What', 'Where', 'Why', 'When', 'Who'. For example, 'what colour is the sky?'. Keep your questions short, clear and simple. A general piece of advice when undertaking any form of advocacy is less is more. Do not ask questions for the sake of it.

Where you are acting in person, you cannot examine yourself in chief. However, the legal advisor or the Judge will normally allow you an opportunity, prior to being cross-examined by the other side, to set out anything that is unclear from your witness statement, anything new you wish to rely on or to set out your position if it has changed since your witness statement was prepared.

You will, however, examine in chief any witnesses whom you are calling to give evidence. When you call one of your witnesses to give evidence you should start by asking them to give their name, occupation and address to the Court (unless that address is confidential).

You should refer them to their witness statement, which should be in the court bundle, and refer them to the first page of the statement. Then ask them to confirm that it is their statement and to turn to the page where they have signed the Statement of Truth. Ask them to confirm that this is their signature and that the statement is true to their knowledge and belief. You should also get them to confirm the truth of all and any exhibits.

Do not be surprised if the Judge or Legal Advisor assists you with this. However, once it has been completed, it is your opportunity to examine them in chief, if you have any questions to ask them.

BEING CROSS-EXAMINED

Being cross-examined is rarely a pleasant experience. You are sitting in a courtroom or Chambers and someone, perhaps your ex-partner or perhaps a lawyer, is firing questions at you. It is something that will make anyone nervous. However, the Court is there to protect you if the questioner crosses the line in their questioning. Here are some basic tips for when you are being cross-examined:

Listen carefully to the question. If you did not hear or understand a word or phrase ask for it to be simplified or repeated.

Answer the question that is actually being asked. Do not answer the question that you think they are going to ask next or the question that you would like to answer. Leave that to the politicians. This is about you being asked questions and Judges do not like it when witnesses come across as too clever, arrogant or purposefully obstructive.

Less is more. Answer in a clear and concise fashion. Nothing else – just answer the actual question. Here is a common example. A witness was once asked, 'Do you have any children?' The witness responded with, 'Yes, I have three children: Johnny, who is ten, Peter, is eight and Mary, who is coming up to five on the twenty-eighth of March.' A perfect answer you might think. But go back to the question: 'Do you have any children?' It is a simple question with a simple, precise answer. In the example above the answer would be 'Yes'. Less is more when you are being cross-examined.

Do not ask questions of the questioner. Your role is simply to answer questions and nothing more. This can be viewed unfavourably by the Court and can come across as being arrogant or unhelpful. It also misunderstands the purpose of giving evidence.

Always remember to think about the child. This is about the subject child or children in the case and your answers, where possible, should bear this in mind. Think about the Welfare

Checklist when you give your answers. Do not get into a row with your opponent or rehash every row that you had prior to the relationship breaking down.

Skilled advocates are very clever when they ask questions and will try to suggest things to you that will help their client's case. So be careful and if they say something that you do not agree with, then make that very clear to them in your answer.

Tell the truth. It is basic but once you start lying you will inevitably be found out.

HOW TO CROSS-EXAMINE

Cross-examination is the process of asking questions of your opponent and their witnesses. The aim of cross-examination is firstly to put your own case to your opponent and secondly to undermine their case. You are now allowed to ask leading questions (using the example from above – the sky is blue, isn't it?). This is a good tactic to put your case to the witness and to try to steer them to say what you want them to say.

It is very sensible to write down your questions in advance of the hearing. This will provide you with structure and hopefully prevent you from getting tongue-tied or from forgetting things. It is about presenting your case or position in its best light. Look for gaps in your opponent's evidence where they are silent about something that they would or should have mentioned. Look for inconsistencies from what they have written in their witness statements and from what they are now saying or from what you know to be the truth. Also, if they have witnesses, highlight inconsistencies in their evidence. In family cases one of the advantages when it comes to cross-examination is that you will generally know your opponent (witness) better than anyone else so you will have the inside track when it comes to asking them questions. If they are lying or being evasive in an answer you will be able to flag this up. If you are worried about speaking to them directly or how to word a question then you can ask the Judge or the legal advisor to put the question to the witness on your behalf. It is for the witness to answer questions, not to ask you questions. Do not become engaged in an argument so be polite and courteous to the witness. Keep it simple, clear and concise.

This is your opportunity to question them about their proposals for the child and if you think that these proposals are wrong or ill-conceived then this is your chance to put these things to the witness.

If the CAFCASS report supports what you are saying then you may wish to refer the witness to this document and particular paragraphs in your questioning. Always consider the Welfare Checklist in your questioning.

RE-EXAMINATION

After your witness has been cross-examined by the other party you are allowed to re-examine them to deal with anything from their evidence that may now be unclear. The purpose of re-examination is to clarify and explain answers given in cross-examination, not just to repeat points. Many lawyers do not undertake re-examination because they think that it just draws attention to weaknesses in that witness's evidence. When re-examining you are only allowed to ask questions arising from the cross-examination and you are still not allowed to ask leading questions.

When you have finished your re-examination the District Judge and/or Magistrates may ask questions of the witnesses, if they have not asked questions before.

SUBMISSIONS

After the Court has heard all the evidence in the case, it allows both parties an opportunity to make a final statement to the Court, which is called submissions. This is when the parties put forward their best arguments to the Court for the Order that they seek. It is also an opportunity to criticise the case of the other party. Mostly the Court will move from hearing evidence to immediately hearing submissions. You may wish to ask the Court for a short five-minute adjournment to allow you to reflect on the evidence and get your thoughts in order.

When preparing your submissions it is a good idea to think about the powers that the Court actually has, and, in particular, the Welfare Checklist. Consider what Order you wish the Court to make and why. The Respondent makes their submissions first and then the Applicant makes their submissions. This is a good time to refer to any parts of the evidence that you think help your case. If you are asking the Court to disregard the recommendations of CAFCASS, this is your opportunity to set out the reasons for this. You can refer to their evidence and any points that you raised in your cross-examination. You can comment upon the presentation of any witness and the manner in which they gave their evidence (for example, you could say that a witness was hostile or evasive). Your closing submissions should:

Be child focused.

Be balanced in the points that you seek to make – try to be fair. Deal if you can with both the positives and the negatives in your opponent's case but say why the Court should do what you want it to do.

Give a summary of why you disagree with the other party's position.

Set out your proposals in a clear and succinct fashion.

Give your position on the CAFCASS report or any other significant evidence.

Take the Court through the elements of the Welfare Checklist and why you say it supports your position or proposals.

If you are the Applicant it is always worthwhile dealing with any points of significance arising from the Respondent's submissions (e.g. if evidence which supports your case has been criticised, you should try to address this).

The Court may ask either party questions arising from their submissions. Then they will usually ask for a short period of time so that they can consider the issues and draft their decisions. In a Final Hearing before Magistrates they will normally seek a few hours to come to their decision and draft their facts and reasons. This is a formal judgment, which sets out the reasoning behind their decision and the facts that they have relied upon in coming to this decision. A District Judge will still need to consider matters before giving a judgment, but can normally give a decision quite quickly.

Can I Vary a Court Order?

A Court can be asked to vary Orders it has made. This may be
appropriate where, for example, contact was to take place between
5 and 7 p.m. on a Tuesday and after that Order was made, your
job changed and that date and time is now not possible, or where
contact was ordered to take place in a particular setting, but having
tried it, you find that the child isn't settling. You would do this by
making a new application on a C100 if the case has finished, or by
a C2 if the case is still going on.

17

Making an Appeal

If a decision that you disagree with is made in a case, it is natural for you to want to consider an appeal. However, just because you feel you 'lost', it does not mean that you can automatically ask a different Judge to consider your case afresh. To successfully make any appeal you need to have 'grounds'.

The starting point will always be to consider the Court's judgment or 'facts and reasons'.

For the vast majority of children cases, there is no one, single right answer. There is only a band of decisions that could be considered reasonable. Because of this, it can be difficult to prove that the Judge got it wrong. Even if the decision you want to object to is not one that other Judges would have made, you may still lose your appeal if the decision was one that is still justified on the facts of the case.

The Judge or Judges in the Appeal Court will not have had the benefit of seeing how the witnesses in the first hearing gave evidence. This makes it difficult for a party to appeal the results of Finding of Fact Hearings that are based on how the witnesses appeared.

If you are unhappy with a decision, you need to ask yourself firstly why you are unhappy and where you feel the Judge went wrong. Try to do this calmly. You will need to think carefully and objectively about the decision to help you decide the right thing to do. Appeals must not be done lightly and there can be costs implications for bringing appeals that are not successful, so you need to be really sure that the decision you wish to appeal is definitely within the category of 'wrong' decisions.

Parties do not come into an appeal with a 'clean sheet'. The Court will not look at the evidence and decide it all over again. The focus of the appeal will instead be whether the Judge or Magistrates got it wrong.

The system for appeals in England and Wales can be complicated. This book is intended to cover the most straightforward types of appeal. If your issues are not covered here, you can get guidance as to the appropriate court forms to use from the court office, but you would be strongly advised to seek legal advice, even if only in the form of a conference with a Solicitor or Barrister acting on a public access basis. This could save you time and court fees.

You can appeal a case if there has been an error of fact, an error of law or a serious procedural or other irregularity by the Judge or Magistrates. The test for appeal when you rely on an error of law or fact is whether the Judge or Magistrates were 'plainly wrong' unless you can argue that your case involved issues of the right to family life and a fair trial, in which case the test can be if the Judge was 'wrong'.

The exact procedure for appeals is set out in Part 30 of the Family Procedure Rules and its practice direction. A Practice Direction is guidance given by a senior Judge about aspects of children cases.

APPLYING FOR PERMISSION TO APPEAL

Depending on the Court that made the Order, you may or may not need to apply for permission to appeal. You do not need permission to appeal if the matter was heard by Magistrates but you will need permission if it was heard by a District Judge or Circuit Judge. Appeals from Magistrates in the Family Court are heard by Circuit Judges.

Appeals against the decisions of District Judges are heard by Circuit Judges. Permission is needed to appeal the decisions and this should be sought first. If the District Judge at the hearing refuses permission, then you can apply to the Circuit Judge for permission.

If you need to apply for permission to appeal, you will need to do this in front of the Judge who made the original decision. This is usually best done at the time the Judgment in dispute is given.

After the Judge has given their judgment you can ask for clarification if there is anything you are unclear about. If you are looking to appeal because the Judge missed something out in their judgment, the better way to deal with it can be to draw it to the Judge's attention at the hearing. This can prevent the need for an appeal if the Judge corrects it at the time.

If you have asked for clarification on the Judgment and you still want to apply, you need to then ask for permission.

202/ HOW TO REPRESENT YOURSELF IN THE FAMILY COURT

When you ask for permission to appeal, you need to give reasons why you want to appeal. This can be, for example, that the Judge put too much weight on one particular factor or did not give enough weight to another.

When you apply for permission to appeal, the Judge can do one of three things. Permission can be granted. Permission can be refused. In both of those instances, the Judge will need to give reasons for the decision. Finally, the Judge can adjourn the application for permission to another day (but in most cases, the question is dealt with then and there).

If permission is refused in front of the Judge you wish to appeal, you can apply for permission to the next level of court.

The test for permission is whether there is a 'reasonable prospect of success' for the appeal. You can ask for a few minutes to get your thoughts in order and think about the judgment before you make the application. Making a careful note of any judgment can help you think about what arguments you can make.

If you seek to appeal a decision, asking for permission to appeal alone will not stop the Order you disagree with from being carried into effect. If you want to stop the Order being carried into effect until an appeal is heard, you will also need to apply for a 'stay'. This basically suspends the Order in dispute. You will need an arguable case for this to be considered by the Court.

THE PROCEDURE FOR APPEAL

Any party to the case can appeal (if they have grounds), and the Court's refusal to make an Order can be challenged just as much as any Order the Court chooses to make.

If permission to appeal is required, it is usual for that to be applied for on the day the decision in question is handed down, i.e. immediately after the Judge gives you his decision. You will be asked to give reasons why you are seeking to appeal.

If you are successful in obtaining permission to appeal, the Court will give directions for you to prepare and file your Notice of Appeal. If you are unsuccessful and the Judge does not set a specific deadline to make a new application, then you have 21 days from the date of the decision to file your Notice of Appeal if you intend to appeal the decision of Magistrates, a District Judge or a Circuit Judge. It is possible to apply for leave to appeal outside of these time limits but it is not guaranteed that a Judge would allow this. It would depend on your reasons for delay. Your Notice of Appeal must be served on the Court and parties no later than 7 days after it was filed.

If you do not have permission to appeal, you need to apply for permission to the Court you are appealing to and this can be set out in your Notice of Appeal. Your Notice needs to set out the 'grounds' you rely on for your appeal, namely the reasons why you say the Judge made an error. It helps to list and number these reasons.

In the Court of Appeal, although those responding to the appeal will be given notice of when the application for permission will be heard, they will not be required to attend unless invited.

Preparing a chronology of relevant events can be very helpful. Once you have filed your Notice of Appeal, it cannot be amended without permission.

NOTICE OF APPEAL

You need to serve your Notice of Appeal on the other parties and CAFCASS if a report was prepared. If you are appealing the decision of Magistrates in the Family Court, you need to also serve it on the court officer.

At the same time as filing your Notice of Appeal, or as soon as possible afterwards (no later than 14 days), you need to file a skeleton argument. This is a written document expanding on your Notice of Appeal, setting out the arguments you want to raise. You also need to provide a sealed (i.e. original, with the court seal) copy of the Order you are appealing, and the Order refusing you permission to appeal (if relevant) and the reasons for doing so. You should also provide any witness statements you are relying on. You will also need to provide enough copies of your Notice for the Court and the respondents. You will also need to consider if you need to apply to 'stay' or suspend the Order you want to appeal.

You will also need to get a transcript of the judgment you are appealing, particularly if the Judge did not give you a copy of their judgment in writing, or copies of the Justices' Facts and Reasons. There can be a cost involved in getting a transcript and the Judge you are appealing will need to approve the transcript before it is used. You will need to meet the deadlines set out by the Court. Therefore, transcripts need to be sought early but you may have to begin your appeal without them. You can ask later for permission to amend your grounds if the transcript raised other issues. It is therefore always good practice to make a note of any judgment while it is being read out.

You will be required to provide the Court with bundles containing all of the above documents, together with any other papers (ideally agreed with the other side) from the case that are relevant.

RESPONDING TO AN APPEAL

If you are responding to an appeal, you can file a Respondent's Notice within 14 days, unless the Court provides a different timescale. This can allow you to set out your response, although you will have another opportunity to do that later on. In particular, you will be asked to file your own skeleton argument. You file a Respondent's Notice if you want the decision to be upheld for different reasons than those given by the Judge.

The timescales for preparing and serving bundles will vary depending on the Court you are appealing to. You should check in your case with the relevant court office or the practice direction if you are not sure.

On an appeal, if permission is granted, the Court can allow the appeal, dismiss it, or send it back to the lower court for rehearing. Appeal hearings rarely involve oral evidence. They will usually take the form of speeches in front of the Judge explaining the issues taken with the decision. The Court will not take into account new evidence without an application.

18

Section 91 (14) Children Act 1989

This is often referred to as a 'Barring Order'. The Court has the power under this section to restrict people from making applications to the Court unless the Court gives them permission (or leave) to make such an application. Where there have been repeated and unreasonable applications by a person then the Court can as a matter of last resort use this somewhat draconian power to prevent them from making further application, unless they can prove to the Court that there has been a genuine and substantial change in circumstances. Section 91(14)s can be made either on application by a party or the Court on its own motion. It is a power used only sparingly by the Court with great care.

Such an Order can also be made if it is in the child's best interests for another reason, even if the applications that have been made have not been particularly repetitive or unreasonable. It may be that a case has gone on for so long (and so only one application has actually been made but there have been many, many hearings) that the child is felt to need a break from any further court cases.

Although children are directly involved in coming to court on only a very, very few occasions, it is clear that they can be affected by litigation. They may feel uncertainty as to what is going to happen to them and be upset that their parents are not getting on. Section 91(14) Orders can be used to protect them from this.

The Court must say how long the Order will last for. It is clear that the Court should not make such an Order unless both parties have been given advance warning and an opportunity to tell the Court what they think about the proposed Order. The Court would normally grant a request for a short adjournment to consider the position, where necessary. The application for leave would be made on Form C2. If leave is granted, the application would proceed under the normal route under Form C1.

The effect of the Order is not to deny individuals who have good cases access to the Courts. It is simply used as a filter to prevent, in the appropriate cases, the child from being further involved in proceedings.

19

Enforcement of Orders

If a parent does not comply with a Court Order, it is possible to apply to the Court for the Order to be enforced.

ENFORCING CHILD ARRANGEMENTS ORDERS

You can enforce those parts of a Child Arrangements Order that place an obligation on a particular person to either do something, or to refrain from doing something.

A Child Arrangements Order can require a parent to make a child available to spend time with the other parent. This is a positive obligation and can be enforced. If the parent due to spend time with that child fails to attend, it is not possible to launch enforcement proceedings for that aspect unless the Order (unusually) obliges them to attend. The issue of a parent failing to attend contact is often best addressed by applying to the Court to vary or discharge (end) the Order requiring the child to be made available.

The first thing to check is whether there is a 'Contact Warning Notice' on the Order. It is this paragraph that gives the Court power to punish people who do not comply. If there is no Warning Notice, a first step may be to apply to the Court for one to be added.

The Contact Warning Notice usually appears on the Order below any Child Arrangements Order and will explain that if the Order is not complied with a person may be fined or imprisoned for breaching it.

The key to any enforcement hearing is to look firstly at whether the Order was complied with or breached, and secondly, whether there was a reasonable excuse for not doing so.

It is possible for the Court to decide that the Order was not complied with but there is no enforceable breach because there was good reason.

For example:

> *A Court Order requires Miss Perkins to take Jake (3) for contact to his father, Mr White, every Saturday for two hours. Mr White states that Jake was not taken to contact last week. Miss Perkins says that Jake had chicken pox and was kept at home on doctor's advice.*

In this case, there is on the face of it a breach of the Order because Jake was not taken to see his father, but the reason of Jake's ill health is likely to mean that there will be no punishment.

However, if it was the case that Jake was kept at home because Miss Perkins did not want to take him on those days, then this is likely to be taken as a breach of the Order without good reason.

If an older child starts to become distressed about going to spend time with a parent and cannot be persuaded to attend, it is often sensible for the parent who is not complying with the Court Order to try to bring the case back to court for an urgent hearing to vary the Order, rather than to continue to not take the child regularly, unless the other parent agrees to a temporary break in contact and therefore to suspend the Order.

The Court does have the power to imprison parents who do not comply with Court Orders. Do not assume that this will not apply in your particular case. Judges have imprisoned parents who have not complied, and this has included parents who are the main carers of children. Equally, imprisonment is not the only way, or even the most common way of enforcing Orders. The Court can instead look at issuing fines or unpaid work.

If you find yourself responding to an application for enforcement of a Contact Order, this is a serious situation. It is essential that you try to obtain legal advice. Your liberty could be at stake and you will want to make sure that you are able to respond properly to the application.

The Court should give you an opportunity to respond firstly to the allegation that you have breached the Order and, secondly, if you are found to have breached the Order, you should be allowed to set out your case in relation to the sentence you should receive.

ENFORCEMENT OF A SPECIFIC ISSUE OR PROHIBITED STEPS ORDER

Contact Warning Notices apply strictly to Orders making a child available to spend time with a parent. Prohibited Steps Orders and

Specific Issue Orders are enforced differently. The first step to enforce these types of Orders is to get a Penal Notice attached to the Order. This Penal Notice is very similar to a Contact Warning Notice in that it again explains that if a person breaches the Order, they can be punished by way of imprisonment or a fine.

Again, the Court will have to consider firstly if there has been a breach, and secondly any relevant circumstances that should be taken into account before sentence is passed.

PROCEDURE FOR ENFORCEMENT

Enforcement proceedings of any type are serious and can lead to a person losing their liberty. Therefore, it is important that all of the correct steps are taken to bring the case to court. The process is designed to make sure that the person facing the enforcement application has clear notice of what they are said to have done wrong, and a chance to respond.

A person found to be in breach of a Contact Order may be fined, imprisoned, or ordered to do unpaid work. It is also the case that financial compensation can be sought by the parent who proved the breach for monies lost as a result of the cancelled contact.

The main thing to remember is that the Court is going to be asked to punish a parent for breaking a Court Order and this punishment can include imprisonment. It is therefore really important that you fill out the paperwork carefully and set out exactly what breach of the Order you say has taken place.

At the first hearing of the application, the Court will look at whether the breaches are admitted or denied and whether the case can be dealt with at that time. If the breaches are not admitted, it is likely that the case will need to be decided at a trial. It will be the job of the Court at the first hearing to decide what evidence is needed for a trial, when it should be filed and served and how long any enforcement hearing will take.

Sometimes one party will apply for enforcement at the same time or just before the other party applies to vary the Contact Order. If that is the case, it is likely that both applications will be heard together and the Court will then decide whether the Order was breached in the past as alleged and whether the Order needs to be changed.

Just because an Order is changed does not mean that breaches of the old Order are irrelevant or cannot be enforced.

BRINGING ENFORCEMENT PROCEEDINGS – THINGS TO ASK YOURSELF

◆ Am I trying to enforce an Order that is capable of being enforced? Does the Order require a person to do (or not do) a specific action? Is there a Penal Notice or a Contact Warning Notice in force?

◆ Can I prove that the person I want to take proceedings against was aware of the Order and the Notice? Can you show that they were present in court, or served with the Order and was the importance of the Notice explained to them?

◆ What do I want to achieve from the proceedings? Enforcement proceedings are unlikely to improve relations between you and the parent responding to the application. Is this the right step for your case? Is it a last resort?

- Do I also want to vary the existing Order? If you do, then you need to consider whether you need to make this as a separate application in addition to the application for enforcement.

- What evidence do I have to support the breaches? You will bear the burden of proving beyond reasonable doubt that the Order was breached without reasonable excuse. What explanation has been given? Is there evidence to support the other party's case that you need to take into account?

- Have I set the breaches out clearly enough in the papers? The person responding to your application needs to know exactly what it is they are said to have done and the times and dates of the breaches.

RESPONDING TO ENFORCEMENT PROCEEDINGS – THINGS TO ASK YOURSELF

- Did I comply with the Order? Do I need to make any admissions?

- What evidence can I bring to defend the application? Is there evidence, for example, that your child was unwell and could not go to contact? Did you give notice of the change to contact to the other parent? Is there evidence of this; for example, a text message?

- Did I receive the Order and the relevant Notices? Were the consequences of breach explained to me?

There are times when contact is stopped because a parent is worried about the child's welfare when visiting their other parent. These situations are often very tense and difficult and it is important if you find yourself in a position of wanting to stop contact that you act properly, particularly if there is a Court Order.

Firstly, think carefully about the welfare concerns you have. Are they sufficiently serious to justify stopping contact without the Court approving a change in the Court Order? If you are concerned, for example, that the other parent is always late for contact, this is possibly not as urgent as having to stop contact because you are concerned that the child will be physically hurt in some way if it takes place.

Secondly, consider informing the other parent first and trying to resolve the issue that way. This can prevent the acrimony of more court proceedings and if they agree to a change in contact, this can mean that the case doesn't need to come back to court.

Thirdly, what advice have you been able to get from professionals? If you have serious welfare concerns that you feel justify stopping contact, you may wish to consider getting advice from Social Services, for example. If the advice you receive supports you stopping contact urgently, this is important information that can help you if you are later faced with an enforcement application.

PROCEDURE

Applications for enforcement are brought on Form C79. As with all other court forms, these are available online or through your local Court Office. You will need to serve the Order on the person you allege to be in breach. If contact is being monitored by CAFCASS under a Monitoring Order, or your child was a party to proceedings and had a CAFCASS Guardian, you will also need to give notice to CAFCASS. You use Form C6 to give Notice of Proceedings and you will serve that form on both the party you say is in breach and also CAFCASS, where you are required to.

You need to serve the Application and any Notices no later than 14 days before the first hearing, although the Court can shorten this time in urgent cases.

If you are served with an application for enforcement, you must file an acknowledgement of service in Form C7 no later than 14 days after you are served. This therefore must be done before the date of the listed hearing.

Any Order made by the Court needs to be served by the person who applied for the Order on CAFCASS and the other party as soon as practicable after the hearing. The other party must be served personally with the Order.

If you decide not to pursue your application for enforcement, you will need to get the Court's permission to withdraw. This is because the case will have been based on non-compliance with the Orders of the Court. It is therefore for the Court to decide how its own Orders should be policed. You will usually make the application to withdraw the application at a short hearing.

OTHER OPTIONS

There are other options in respect of ensuring contact is complied with. The Court can make a Contact Monitoring Order requiring CAFCASS to monitor compliance for a set period of time (up to a year) and report to the Court at the end of that time. This can be a useful tool to monitor contact.

Appendix 1: Draft Court Orders

Order at FHDRA/Directions – Child Arrangements Programme

In the Family Court   **Case No**
Sitting at [*place*]

The Children Act 1989

THE CHILDREN

Names	Girl /Boy	Dob.

Order - First Hearing Dispute Resolution Appointment (FHDRA)/directions (CAP 02)
[*Sequential number in these proceedings*]

HHJ/DJ/AJC [*NAME OF JUDGE*]   **SITTING IN OPEN COURT/PRIVATE ON**
[*DATE*]

1. **THE PARTIES**
   The applicant (mother/father/as appropriate) is [*name*]
   The [first] respondent (father/mother/as appropriate) is [*name*]
   [The second respondent (child(ren) through their children's guardian) [*name*]]

2. The child/ren is/are living with ....

3. **NOTICE**
   Today's hearing is on notice/not on notice/on short notice..[*give details*]

4. **REPRESENTATION AT THIS HEARING**
   The parties appeared before the court as follows:

Party/Name	In Person	Counsel/Solicitor/ Advocate	Contact telephone and email address
Applicant			
Respondent(s) (1) (2)			
Other (specify)			

CAP02 Order at FHDRA Directions – version 1.1 May 2014

Order at FHDRA/Directions – Child Arrangements Programme

The names of the children set out in the heading to this Order and the names of the persons set out in paragraphs 3 are not to be disclosed in public without the permission of the court.

5. ALLOCATION / TRANSFER

The proceedings are today/continue to be allocated to be heard by [lay justices / District Judge / Circuit Judge / High Court Judge] and are reserved to [.....................]

This application is transferred to the [Family Court sitting at   ]

6. Cafcass / CAFCASS Cymru

The court has decided that a Cafcass/ CAFCASS Cymru investigation and report is not required in this case
or The Court has appointed a Cafcass / CAFCASS Cymru officer.
If the identity of the Cafcass / CAFCASS Cymru officer is known at this stage:
The Cafcass / CAFCASS Cymru officer is:-
Name
Professional address
Date of appointment

7. THE APPLICATION(S)

(a) The applicant has applied for a Child Arrangements Order/Specific Issue Order/Prohibited Steps Order other Part II order *[delete as appropriate or specify]* *[today / on date]*
(b) *[If there are other applications add as follows or delete]*
(c) The [mother/father/as appropriate] has applied for [   ] *[today / on date]*

8. SAFEGUARDING CHECKS

(a) The safeguarding checks by Cafcass/CAFCASS Cymru are/are not complete
(b) The safeguarding checks show no safety issues/that the safety issues are.........../that the safety issues are not yet known *[delete as appropriate or specify]*

9. TODAY'S HEARING

   a. Today's hearing is listed as a *[FHDRA / directions hearing]*
   b. Today's hearing has been [EFFECTIVE AS THE FINAL HEARING] [EFFECTIVE AS THE FHDRA] [EFFECTIVE AS A DIRECTIONS HEARING] [CANCELLED] [ADJOURNED]
   c. The reason why the hearing has been adjourned is: [*specify*]

10. TIMETABLE FOR THE CHILD(REN)

The key dates and events in the timetable for the child are [..............].

11. KEY ISSUES

A. The issues about which the parties are agreed are:-

Order at FHDRA/Directions – Child Arrangements Programme

a)	
b)	
c)	
d)	

B. The issues which remain to be resolved are:-

a)	
b)	
c)	
d)	

C. The steps planned to resolve the issues are:-
[where the parties intend to refer themselves to mediation or other form of non-court dispute resolution if appropriate]

a)	
b)	
c)	
d)	

12. FACT FINDING

Having considered the documents, received the representations of the parties, and the safeguarding report, a separate fact finding hearing is not necessary in this case because the nature of the allegations [and/or admissions] are such that the court does not require such a hearing in order to be able to decide whether to make the orders sought.
Or
Having considered the documents, received the representations of the parties, and the safeguarding report, a fact finding hearing is necessary in this case because...........
[delete/complete as appropriate]
The issues to be determined are

a)	
b)	
c)	
d)	

13. AGREED [INTERIM] ARRANGEMENTS FOR THE CHILDREN
If determined at this hearing, specify, such as:-

- [Between now and [date/the final hearing] the agreed arrangements for the child[ren] will be

Order at FHDRA/Directions – Child Arrangements Programme

[as set out in the schedule to this order *(if extensive)* / as follows…].

- [Between now and [date/the final hearing]] the child[ren] will live with the [mother/father].
- [Between now and [date/the final hearing]] the children will live with the mother and the father.
- [Between now and [date/the final hearing]], the child[ren] will spend time or otherwise have contact with the [mother/father] as follows/ as set out in the schedule to this order *(if extensive)*.
- [Between now and [date/the final hearing]], the child[ren] will have indirect contact as [follows/ as set out in the schedule to this order *(if extensive)*.

14. UNDERTAKINGS
Record as appropriate

THE COURT ORDERS:

15. JOINDER OF CHILD[REN]/OTHER PARTIES/INTERVENERS
(a) The child[ren] [*name*] shall forthwith be made [a party/parties] to the proceedings and pursuant to rule 16.4 and PD16A, Part 4 FPR 2010 an officer of Cafcass/ CAFCASS Cymru shall be appointed to act as [his/her/their] children's guardian.

(b) A copy of this order shall be faxed/e-mailed to the Cafcass/CAFCASS Cymru office and a hard copy of this order shall be sent within two working days of this order.

(c) The service manager [is requested / has agreed to] allocate an officer as children's guardian as promptly as possible following receipt of this order, and to notify the court within 7 days of such allocation.

(d) It is recorded that there are [no] reasons why the Cafcass officer / WFPO dealing with the case should not continue to deal with it as guardian.

(e) In the event that Cafcass/CAFCASS Cymru is unable to provide a children's guardian to act within [28 days] they shall notify the court forthwith, to enable the court to consider the appointment of another person.

16. CHILD ARRANGEMENTS
[if made at this hearing, specify as appropriate]
Such as:

- It is ordered [by consent] that [between the date of this order and.../the date of the next hearing/final disposal of the applications] the arrangements for the child[ren] shall be [as set out in the schedule to this order *(if extensive)*/as follows...*[specify]*: e.g. the child[ren] shall live with / spend time / indirect contact with [name] by way of [Skype/Facetime/telephone etc]]

- It is ordered that [a warning notice will be endorsed][by consent] [that between the date of this order and [the next hearing/final disposal of the applications] the [father/mother] shall make the child[ren] available to [spend time] / [have indirect contact] with the [father/mother] as set out in the schedule to this order *(if extensive)*/as follows...*[specify]*

A warning notice directed to the [father/mother] shall attach to paragraph [   ] of this order.

Order at FHDRA/Directions – Child Arrangements Programme

17. PARENTAL RESPONSIBILITY

Further to the Child Arrangements Order made [*today/date*], which provides that the child is to live with [the father, who does not currently have parental responsibility] / [*woman* who is a parent of the child by virtue of section 43 of the Human Fertilisation and Embryology Act 2008, without parental responsibility], the court grants parental responsibility to [the father] / [*the woman*].

Further to the Child Arrangements Order made [*today/date*], which provides that the child is to spend time or otherwise have contact (but not live) with [the father, who does not currently have parental responsibility] / [*woman* who is a parent of the child by virtue of section 43 of the Human Fertilisation and Embryology Act 2008, without parental responsibility], the court grants parental responsibility to [the father] / [*the woman*].

Further to the Child Arrangements Order made [*today/date*], which provides that the child is to live with [*a person who is not the parent or guardian of the child concerned is named in the order as a person with whom the child is to spend time or otherwise have contact but not live*] the court grants parental responsibility for the child for as long as the order is in place.

Further to the Child Arrangements Order made [*today/date*], which provides that the child is to spend time or otherwise have contact (but not live) with [*a person who is not the parent or guardian of the child concerned is named in the order as a person with whom the child is to spend time or otherwise have contact but not live*] the court grants parental responsibility for the child for as long as the order is in place.

18. ACTIVITY DIRECTIONS/CONDITIONS
[if made at this hearing, specify as appropriate]
Such as:-
The [father/mother] [other party] is directed to take part in:

Set out any order for Activity Direction/Condition [e.g. Separated Parents Information Programme/ Mediation Information and Assessment Meeting]
on such dates and times as are specified by.......[*the provider*]

The Court shall forthwith send this order to the provider.

The provider shall notify the Court whether the parties attended at the conclusion of the Separated Parents Information Programme/mediation directed

19. CASE MANAGEMENT AND OTHER ORDERS/DIRECTIONS
(a) **Safeguarding incomplete**: Cafcass / CAFCASS Cymru must write to the court by [*date*] with the outcome of safeguarding checks / the case is adjourned to [date] (the parties' attendance is excused) when the court will either make an order in the terms agreed by the parties or list the case for further consideration.

(b) **Sending and delivering of evidence**
    (i) *[specify what is to be sent and delivered by each party]*
    (ii) With this order, the mother/father will be provided with a witness statement
        template relevant for a case concerning:
          • allegations of domestic abuse;

Order at FHDRA/Directions – Child Arrangements Programme

- allegations of child harm;
- where the child is to live and who the child is to see (and when);
- schooling issues;
- temporary or permanent relocation from the jurisdiction.

(iii) By 16:00hs [   ], the Applicant shall file in court and serve on all parties (and Cafcass / CAFCASS Cymru / Local Authority) his/her concise witness statement/s which are signed and contain a statement of truth.

(iv) By 16:00hs on [   ], the Respondent shall file in court and serve on all parties (and Cafcass / CAFCASS Cymru / Local Authority) his/her concise witness statement/s which are signed and contain a statement of truth

(v) The statements shall only contain evidence relevant to the issue/s to be determined and shall set out the terms of any Order they invite the court to make and their reasons for it.

(c) Fact finding Schedules

(i)   The parties have prepared, with the assistance of the court at this hearing, a document setting out the concise schedule of the allegations on which the [mother/father] relies, and [the father/mother]'s answers to the allegations, for the purposes of the fact finding hearing;

(ii)   The [mother/father] shall, by 16:00 on [date], send/deliver to the [father/mother] and to the court a concise schedule of allegations on which [s]he relies for the purpose of the fact finding hearing.

(iii)   The [father/mother] shall, by 16:00 on [date] send/deliver to the [mother/father] and to the court a concise schedule of the answer(s) to the allegations relied on for the purpose of the fact finding hearing.

(d) Disclosure from Police / Medical records

(i)   Cafcass/CAFCASS Cymru are requested to initiate enhanced checks of the relevant local police force, in particular in respect of their investigation into [incident] on [date] and shall send/deliver any relevant information that is received to the [father or mother] and the court.

(ii)   The [solicitor for the] [mother/father] shall seek disclosure of any Force Wide Incident Notices/Sleuth Reports (FWINs) in respect of the parties for the following addresses and for the following periods in accordance with the Police Protocol:

    a. From [   ] to [   ] at the address:
    b. From [   ] to [   ] at the address:

and shall send/deliver the resulting disclosure to the [father/mother] and the court on receipt.

(iii)   The [solicitor for the] [mother/father] shall seek disclosure from the police of any statements / reports / notes of interview relevant to their investigation into [incident] on [date], in accordance with the Police Protocol and shall send/deliver the resulting disclosure to the [father/mother] and the court on receipt.

(iv)   The Court considering it both necessary and proportionate so to order for there to be a proper determination of the (preliminary) issues, the applicant/respondent has permission to rely on a report/statement from [*Hospital, GP*   ] which must be filed at court and a copy served on the other party by 16:00hs on [
    ].

Order at FHDRA/Directions – Child Arrangements Programme

(v) Permission is granted to [the solicitor for] the applicant/respondent to disclose this order to the record holder. The costs of obtaining the report shall be divided equally between the parties and shall be a proper charge upon the funding certificates of the publicly funded parties.

(d) Cafcass / CAFCASS Cymru / Local Authority s.7 Reports / s.37 investigation and report.
A [Cafcass / CAFCASS Cymru officer / local authority social worker] is directed to prepare a section 7 report on:
Specify as appropriate, such as:-

- The ascertainable wishes and feelings of the children.
- It is recorded that the [mother/father] alleges that the children have expressed a wish that [*specify*]
- The home conditions and suitability of the accommodation of the [mother/father]
- The concerns of the [mother/father] with regard to [*specify*]
- Whether or not the children's physical/emotional/educational needs are being met by the [mother/father]
- How the children will be affected by the proposed change of [*specify*]
- Whether or not it appears that the children have suffered or at risk of suffering the harm alleged by the [mother/father]
- The parenting capacity of the [mother/father] having regard to the allegations that [*specify*]
- Whether [*Specify*] local authority should be requested to report under section 37 Children Act 1989.

A [*named local authority*] is directed to prepare a section 37 report in respect of the child(ren), the Court being of the view that it may be appropriate for a care or supervision order to be made with respect to the child(ren). The authority shall, when advising the court, consider whether they should apply for a care or supervision order, or provide services or assistance to the child(ren), and/or take any further action.

In the event that the Local Authority considers that it is unable to comply with this direction, it shall no later than 16:00hs 3 days after service of this order upon it provide to the court in writing its reasons for holding that view. A copy shall at the same time be sent by email to [*insert email address*]

Permission is given for the Court to release [and send to the Local Authority] the safeguarding screening report by Cafcass to the Department, together with all the applications, statements and orders.

[Cafcass / CAFCASS Cymru / the local authority] shall send the report to the court by 16:00 on [date] and at the same time deliver a copy of the report to each of the parties and, if applicable, to their solicitors.

(e) Disclosure of documents
The following documents are to be disclosed (by sending or delivering such documents) by the mother/father to [Cafcass / CAFCASS Cymru / the local authority with children's services functions of [local authority as appropriate][*list documents to be disclosed*].

Order at FHDRA/Directions – Child Arrangements Programme

(f) Experts

Drug and alcohol testing

The Court considering it both necessary and proportionate so to order for there to be a proper determination of the (preliminary) issues, the [Mother] [and] [Father]/ shall co-operate with scientific hair strand testing for

a. [all prohibited substances]/ [for the following prohibited substances....:..for the   months immediately preceding this order
b. [and] [for excessive alcohol consumption (by FAEE/CDT and EtG testing)] for a ....month period of assessment.
c. It is recorded that the ....   has been advised that any future tests should be carried out on hair from his/her head if at all possible and it is in his/her interests to ensure that it is of sufficient length to enable an effective test to be carried out.
d. a written report as to the results of the tests shall be sent to the court and the parties by 16:00hs on
   ....
e. the costs of the testing shall be shared equally by the parties and shall be a proper charge of the funding certificates of the publicly funded parties

DNA Paternity Testing

The Court considering it both necessary and proportionate so to order for there to be a proper determination of the (preliminary) issues, and pursuant to Section 20 (1) of the Family Law Reform Act 1969, the solicitor for the children may instruct [
            ] to conduct scientific tests to ascertain whether [
            ] is or is not the father of [   ] and the following directions shall apply:-

a. for that purpose bodily samples be taken on or before [   ] from the following persons:
   i. the child:
   ii. The mother:
   iii. The putative father:
b. The person appearing to the court to have care and control of the child is:
c. Arrangements for the provision of samples shall be made by the solicitor for the children;
d. The report regarding the paternity of [   ] shall be served on all other parties by the solicitor for the children by 16:00hs on the   ; and
e. The reasonable fees for the paternity testing shall be divided equally between the parties and shall be a proper charge of the funding certificates of the publicly funded parties

Adult psychiatrist

The Court considering it both necessary and proportionate so to order for there to be a proper determination of the (preliminary) issues, permission is granted to the [
            ] solicitor as nominated lead solicitor to disclose the case papers and

Order at FHDRA/Directions – Child Arrangements Programme

relevant medical records to and to instruct [   ] to undertake a
psychiatric assessment of the   [   ].

    a. The report shall by filed by the lead Solicitor no later than 16:00hs on
       the   [   ] and shall address the following issues:
       i.
    b. The lead solicitor shall forthwith send an electronic copy of this order
       to the expert instructed
    c. The approved letter of instruction and the bundle of documents shall be
       delivered to the expert by not later than 4.00pm on the [
       ]
    d. The reasonable costs incurred in the preparation of this report shall be
       divided equally between the parties and shall be deemed a reasonable
       disbursement upon the publicly funded parties' public funding
       certificates.

Adult psychologist
The Court considering it both necessary and proportionate so to order for there to be a
proper determination of the (preliminary) issues, permission is granted to the [
] solicitor as nominated lead solicitor to disclose the case papers and
relevant medical records to and to instruct [   ] to undertake a
psychological assessment of the   [   ].

    a. The report shall by filed by the lead Solicitor no later than 4.00pm on
       the   [   ] and shall address the following issues:
       i.
    b. The lead solicitor shall forthwith send an electronic copy of this order
       to the expert instructed
    c. The approved letter of instruction and the bundle of documents shall be
       delivered to the expert by not later than 16:00hs on the [
       ]
    d. The reasonable costs incurred in the preparation of this report shall be
       divided equally between the parties and shall be deemed a reasonable
       disbursement upon the publicly funded parties' public funding
       certificates.

General
For the avoidance of doubt, the expert directed above [shall/shall not] have permission to
examine and assess the child[ren]

(g) Special arrangements for witnesses
[The following special arrangements for witnesses shall apply to the evidence of [name of
witness] *[specify]: or* the court will determine at the hearing on [date] whether and, if so,
which special arrangements shall apply in the case of [name witness]].

20. CONTACT CENTRE DIRECTION
The order for supported contact at the [   ] contact centre
is subject to the following conditions for its operation and effect:-

Order at FHDRA/Directions – Child Arrangements Programme

a. The [parties/ solicitors for the [Mother/Father][   ] shall inform the centre co-ordinator of the contents of this order as soon s practicable.

b. The [parties/ solicitors for the parties] shall jointly be responsible for
   i. completing a referral form for the centre co-ordinator and
   ii. providing a copy of this order and any subsisting injunction orders involving the parties to the co-ordinator as soon as practicable and in any event within 2 days of today.

c. Confirmation from the centre co-ordinator that:
   i. the centre is an accredited member of NACCC;
   ii. the referral has been accepted following completion of a preparation for contact interview (which interview is a compulsory requirement of all NACCC centres);
   iii. a vacancy is available or the parties have been allocated a place upon a waiting list (the order for supported contact is suspended during any waiting period until a place is available).

d. The parties and any person permitted to accompany them to the centre shall abide by the rules of the centre.

e. The parties must attend a preparation for contact meeting with the centre co-ordinator (the parties' solicitors, if acting, must take responsibility for ensuring that information about the meeting is passed to the parties).

f. The [Mother/Father] [   ] agrees to take the child(ren) for a pre-contact introductory visit to the centre.

g. The child(ren) will be informed of the contact arrangements by [Mother/Father] [   ]

h. The following arrangements for the contact sessions shall apply:-
   i. The child(ren) shall be taken to the centre by
   ii. The child(ren) shall be collected at the conclusion of contact by
   iii. The [Father/Mother] [   ] may [not] be accompanied during the contact session [by]
   iv. The [Father/Mother] [   ] may [not] remain in the same room as the child(ren) during the contact session
   v. After [*] sessions of contact, the [Father/Mother] [   ] shall not remain in the same room as the child(ren) but may remain in the confines of the centre.
   vi. [Other agreements about contact at the centre]

i. The [parties/ the parties' solicitors] shall jointly be responsible for informing the centre co-ordinator when the place is no longer required.

21. FURTHER HEARINGS
Directions as appropriate, such as:-

(a) [This/These] application[s] shall be listed for [fact-finding hearing/Dispute Resolution Appointment/other directions hearing/final hearing] before [Legal Advisor/Lay Justices/District Judge/Circuit Judge/High Court Judge] [reserved to...] on [date] with a time estimate of [specify] and for final hearing on [date] with a time estimate of [specify].

(b) The author of the [section 7] report [shall not] [shall] be required to attend the Dispute Resolution Appointment;

Order at FHDRA/Directions – Child Arrangements Programme

(c) The author of the [section 7] [section 37] report shall attend the [final/as appropriate] hearing on [date]   unless all parties have confirmed to him/her no less than five days in advance of the hearing date that [his/her] attendance is not required.

(d) The [mother/father] shall by 16:00 on [date] deliver to the court a paginated and indexed trial bundle [and provide a copy to [party/Cafcass/CAFCASS Cymru].

(e) The parties **MUST** arrive at court at least [30 45 60] minutes before any future hearings

22. COSTS

No order as to costs *or*

Costs in the application *or*

Costs reserved *or*

Funded services assessment of the costs of *[specify]or*

Other *[specify]*

23. COMPLIANCE

(a) No document other than a document specified in this order or delivered in accordance with the Rules or any Practice Direction shall be delivered by any party without the court's permission.

(b) Any application to vary this order or for any other order is to be made to the allocated judge on notice to [   ] / all parties.

(c) In the event of non-compliance by any person with any order or direction made today, each party shall be responsible for notifying the court of the same, in order to avoid delay.

Dated

Court address: for filing/communication:

CAP02 Order at FHDRA Directions – version 1.1 May 2014

Order at FHDRA/Directions – Child Arrangements Programme

In the Family Court　　　　　　　**Case No**
sitting at [*place*]

The Children Act 1989

THE CHILDREN

Names	Girl /Boy	Dob.

FHDRA / Directions Hearing Order Number [*Sequential number in these proceedings*]

1. **THE PARTIES AND REPRESENTATION AT THIS HEARING**
   The applicant (mother/father/as appropriate) is [*name*] and is a litigant in person/ represented by [*name of advocate and contact details*]

   The [first] respondent (father/mother/as appropriate) is [*name*] and is a litigant in person/ represented by [*name of advocate and contact details*]

   [*Other – provide full details as above*]

2. The child/ren is/are living with ....

3. **NOTICE**
   Today's hearing is on notice/not on notice/on short notice..[*give details*]

The names of the children set out in the heading to this Order and the names of the persons set out in paragraph 1 are not to be disclosed in public without the permission of the court.

4. **ALLOCATION / TRANSFER**
   The proceedings are today/continue to be allocated to [lay justices / District Judge / Circuit Judge / High Court Judge (insert name)] for case management and hearing

   This application is transferred to the [Family Court sitting at　　　　　　]

5. **THE APPLICATION(S)**
   (a) The applicant has applied for a Child Arrangements Order/Specific Issue Order/Prohibited Steps Order other Part II order [*delete as appropriate or specify*] [*today / on date*]
   (b) [*If there are other applications add as follows or delete*]
   (c) The [mother/father/as appropriate] has applied for [　　　　] [*today / on date*]

Order at FHDRA/Directions – Child Arrangements Programme

6. SAFEGUARDING CHECKS
(a) The safeguarding checks by Cafcass/CAFCASS Cymru are/are not complete
(b) The safeguarding checks show no safety issues/that the safety issues are...........that the safety issues are not yet known *[delete as appropriate or specify]*

7. TIMETABLE FOR THE CHILD(REN)
The key dates and events in the timetable for the child(ren) are
(a) ....
(b) ....

8. KEY ISSUES
A. The issues which have been agreed &/or are to be determined are:- *[specify]*
(a) ....
(b) ....

B. The steps planned to resolve the issues are:-
[include if the parties intend to refer themselves to mediation or other form of non-court dispute resolution if appropriate]
(a) ....
(b) ....

9. AGREED [INTERIM] ARRANGEMENTS FOR THE CHILDREN
(a) *[If determined at this hearing, specify, such as:]* Between now and [date/the final hearing] the agreed arrangements for the child[ren] will be [as set out in the schedule to this order *(if extensive)* / as follows...]
(b) [Between now and [date/the final hearing]] the child[ren] will live with the [mother/father].
(c) [Between now and [date/the final hearing]], the child[ren] will spend time or otherwise have contact with the [mother/father] as follows/ as set out in the schedule to this order *(if extensive)*.

10. OTHER RECITALS AS TO POSITIONS / ISSUES
(a) ......
(b) ....

THE COURT ORDERS:

11. JOINDER OF CHILD[REN]
(a) The child[ren] [*name*] are joined as [a party/parties] to the proceedings and pursuant to rule 16.4 and PD16A, Part 4 FPR 2010 an officer of Cafcass/CAFCASS Cymru shall be appointed to act as [his/her/their] children's guardian.
(b) A copy of this order shall be faxed/e-mailed to the Cafcass/CAFCASS Cymru office and a hard copy of this order shall be sent within two working days of this order.
(c) The service manager [is requested/has agreed to] allocate an officer as children's guardian as promptly as possible following receipt of this order, and to notify the court within 7 days of such allocation.
(d) It is recorded that there are [no] reasons why the Cafcass officer / WFPO dealing with the case should not continue to deal with it as guardian.

Order at FHDRA/Directions – Child Arrangements Programme

(e) In the event that Cafcass/CAFCASS Cymru is unable to provide a children's guardian to act within [28 days] they shall notify the court forthwith, to enable the court to consider the appointment of another person.

12. CHILD ARRANGEMENTS
The following child arrangements order is made
    (a) Until [   ] the children shall live with
    (b) Until [   ] the children shall spend time or otherwise have contact with
    [   ] as follows:-

Warning notice
Where a child arrangements order is in force: if you do not comply with this contact order –
    (a) you may be held in contempt of court and be committed to prison or fined: and/or
    (b) the court may make an order requiring you to undertake unpaid work ("an enforcement order") and/or an order that you pay financial compensation.

13. OTHER CHILDREN ORDERS
(a) **Prohibited Steps Orders**
Until further order [*Identify name*] is forbidden to
    (a) remove the child[ren] from the care of [ ] otherwise than for the purpose of agreed or ordered contact
    (b) remove the child[ren] from the United Kingdom without the written consent of the other parent or permission of the court
    (c) change the child[ren]'s school[s]
    (d) change the child[ren]'s name
    (e) other:

(b) **Specific Issue Orders**
    (a) The child[ren] shall attend [ ] School
    (b) The child[ren] shall be known by the name[s]
    (c) Other:

14. PENAL NOTICE
(a) To [ ]: You must obey the instructions contained in this order. If you do not, you will be guilty of contempt of court and you may be sent to prison, fined or your assets may be seized.

(b) This penal notice is attached to the following paragraphs of this order: paragraph

15. PARENTAL RESPONSIBILITY
The court grants parental responsibility to .....

16. ACTIVITY DIRECTIONS
The court makes an activity direction and the parties are directed to take part in the following programme on dates and at times as are specified by the activity provider
    (a) a Mediation Information and Assessment Meeting

Order at FHDRA/Directions – Child Arrangements Programme

(b) a Separated Parents' Information Programme
(c) a Domestic Violence Perpetrators' Programme

The Court shall forthwith send this order to the provider with the parties' contact details.

The provider shall notify the Court whether the parties attended at the conclusion of the activity directed.

17. CASE MANAGEMENT AND OTHER ORDERS/DIRECTIONS
(a) Safeguarding incomplete:

(a) Cafcass must write to the court by [ ] with the outcome of safeguarding checks;
(b) the case is adjourned to [ ] (when the parties' attendance is excused) when the court will either make an order in the terms agreed by the parties or list the case for further consideration.

(b) Sending and delivering of evidence

(a) The parties must by 4:00 pm on [*insert date*] send to each other, to the court and to Cafcass written statements of the evidence on which they intend to rely. This includes the statements of the parties themselves and of any witness they intend to rely on.
(b) When preparing their statements the parties shall use the witness statement template which shall be provided to them by the court.

(c) Fact finding Schedules

The court considers that a fact finding hearing should take place in this case to determine the following issue(s) [*in summary*] [alleged domestic abuse / alleged harm to the child.............]. In the circumstances, the parties must send to each other and to the court a schedule setting out the allegations on which they rely and (using the same document) their responses to such allegations as follows:

(a) by [*insert time & date*] a schedule of any allegations made by either party
(b) by [*insert time & date*] the other party's response

(d) Disclosure from Police / Medical records

(a) Cafcass are requested to initiate enhanced checks of the relevant local police force, in particular in respect of their investigation into [ ] and shall deliver any relevant information that is received to the parties and the court.
(b) The Chief Constable of [*insert area*] is directed to disclose to [the court / the parties directly....] [*insert number*] copies of all reports, incident logs, statements and interview notes relating to any incidents involving the parties between [*insert dates*]. This order shall be served on the Chief Constable by [*insert time & date*]. The Chief Constable may apply within 7 days of service of this order for it to be varied or discharged.
(c) [*Identify party*] must by 4:00 pm on [*insert date*] obtain and disclose to [*identify party*] his/her GP and any hospital medical records. A copy of this order shall be sent with the request to the record holder. Any fee charged by the record holder shall be paid by [*identify party*]

(e) Cafcass / Local Authority s.7 Reports / s.37 investigation and report.

(a) The court directs a section 7 report by Cafcass / [Local Authority] dealing with the following matters:

Order at FHDRA/Directions – Child Arrangements Programme

(1) The ascertainable wishes and feelings of the children.

(2) The home conditions and suitability of the accommodation of the [mother/father]

(3) The concerns of the [mother/father] with regard to [*specify*]

(4) Whether or not the children's physical/emotional/educational needs are being met by the [mother/father]

(5) How the children will be affected by the proposed change of [*specify*]

(6) Whether or not it appears that the children have suffered or at risk of suffering the harm alleged by the [mother/father/

(7) The parenting capacity of the [mother/father] having regard to the allegations that [*specify*]

(8) Whether [*Specify*] local authority should be requested to report under section 37 Children Act 1989.

(b) [*named local authority*] is directed to prepare a section 37 report in respect of the child(ren), the Court being of the view that it may be appropriate for a care or supervision order to be made with respect to the child(ren). The authority shall, when advising the court, consider whether they should apply for a care or supervision order, or provide services or assistance to the child(ren), and/or take any further action. The court shall send to the local authority preparing the report the application, any C1A and the Cafcass safeguarding letter [together with]

(c) The report shall be sent to the court [and to the parties] by no later than 4:00 pm on [*insert time & date*]

(f) Experts

The Court gives permission for the parties to rely on the following expert evidence. The parties shall take such steps as are necessary to ensure that the expert evidence is obtained and made available to the court in accordance with the directions below, and shall provide any samples that are required for the purpose of testing

(a) Type of expert:

(b) The issues on which the expert is to report are:

(c) The expert is to be instructed by the parties together as a single expert.

(d) The expert is to be instructed by [ ]

(e) A copy of this order must be sent to the expert with the expert's instructions.

(f) Date for delivery of instructions/provision of necessary samples:

(g) Date for delivery of the expert's report:

(h) Any expert's fees shall be paid by [ ]

(i) The expert may [not] see the child[ren] for the purpose of any assessment:

The court gives the following further directions in relation to the obtaining of expert evidence:

18. CONTACT CENTRE DIRECTION

The order for supported contact at the contact centre is subject to the following conditions for its operation and effect:-

(a) [ ] shall inform the centre co-ordinator of the contents of this order as soon as practicable.

(b) The parties shall jointly be responsible for – (i) completing a referral form for the centre co-ordinator; and (ii) providing a copy of this order and any

Order at FHDRA/Directions – Child Arrangements Programme

subsisting injunction orders involving the parties to the co-ordinator as soon as practicable and in any event within 2 days of today.
(c) The parties and any person permitted to accompany them to the centre shall abide by the rules of the centre.
(d) The following arrangements for the contact sessions shall apply:-
    (1) The child(ren) shall be taken to the centre by [ ]
    (2) The child(ren) shall be collected at the conclusion of contact by [ ]
    (3) [ ] may [not] be accompanied during the contact session [by]
    (4) [ ] may [not] remain in the same room as the child(ren) during the contact session
    (5) [Other agreements about contact at the centre]
(e) The parties shall jointly be responsible for informing the centre co-ordinator when the place is no longer required.

19. FURTHER HEARINGS
(a) The next hearing will be a [fact-finding hearing/ Dispute Resolution Appointment/ other directions hearing/final hearing] before [… [Name]] which will take place at [*identify place*] at 10.30 am on [*identify date*]
(b) The author of the [section 7] report shall [not] be required to attend the Dispute Resolution Appointment;
(c) The parties **MUST** arrive at court at least 60 minutes before any future hearings

20. COSTS
No order as to costs *or*
Costs in the application *or*
Costs reserved *or*

21. COMPLIANCE
(a) No document other than a document specified in this order or delivered in accordance with the Rules or any Practice Direction shall be delivered by any party without the court's permission.
(b) Any application to vary this order or for any other order is to be made to the allocated judge on notice to [   ] / all parties.
(c) In the event of non-compliance by any person with any order or direction made today, each party shall be responsible for notifying the court of the same, in order to avoid delay.

Ordered by [*Names*]Lay Justices / District Judge [*Name*] / His Honour Judge/ [*Name*]

Dated:

Court address: for filing/communication:

Final Order – Child Arrangements Programme

In the Family Court   **Case No**
Sitting at *[place]*

The Children Act 1989 – Child Arrangements Programme

THE CHILDREN

Names	Girl /Boy	Dob.

Final Order (CAP 04)

MR/MRS JUSTICE/HHJ[S.9]/DJ/AJC *[NAME OF JUDGE]* **SITTING IN OPEN COURT / PRIVATE ON** *[DATE]*

1. THE PARTIES
The applicant (mother/father/as appropriate) is *[name]*
The first respondent (father/mother/as appropriate) is *[name]*
The second respondent (child/father of/as appropriate) is *[name]*
[The third respondent(s) is/are (the children) by their children's guardian *[name]*]
[The first intervener *[state relationship to child(ren) or other party]* is *[name]*]

2. The child/ren is/are living with....

3. REPRESENTATION AT THIS HEARING
The parties appeared before the court as follows:

Party/Name	In Person	Counsel/Solicitor/ Advocate	Contact telephone and email address
Applicant			
Respondent(s) (1) (2)			
Other (specify)			

Final Order – Child Arrangements Programme

The names set out in paragraph 3 are not to be disclosed in public without the permission of the court.

4. Cafcass / CAFCASS Cymru / Local Authority *[if appointed]*
Name
Professional address
Date of appointment (if children's guardian):
Date of order of [section 7] [section 37] report

5. THE APPLICATIONS
The applicant has applied for a Child Arrangements Order/Specific Issue Order/Prohibited Steps Order/ other Part 2 order *[delete as appropriate or specify]* *[today / on date]*
   [If there are other applications add as follows or delete]
The *[specify party]* has applied for [   ] *[today / on date]*

6. THE HEARING
a.   Today's case was listed for: [*]
b.   Today's hearing has been [EFFECTIVE AS THE FINAL HEARING] [EFFECTIVE] [CANCELLED] [ADJOURNED]
c.   The reason why the hearing has been adjourned is: [*]
The next hearing is a [*] on *[date and time]* at *[court]* with a time estimate of [   ] [this matter is part heard]

7. AGREEMENTS/AGREED ARRANGEMENTS FOR THE CHILDREN
Such as:-
• The child[ren] will live with the [mother/father/mother and father] as set out in the schedule to this order *(if extensive)*/as follows…]
• The [mother/father] agrees to make the child[ren] available to visit/stay with/have indirect contact with the [mother/father] [as set out in the schedule to this order *(if extensive)*/as follows…]
The [mother/father] may remove the child[ren] from England and Wales [for the purposes of a holiday to *[specify]*][to live in   ]. The details of the arrangements for the [holiday/removal from the jurisdiction] are to be [as follows…/ as set out in the schedule to this order *(if extensive)*.

8. UNDERTAKINGS
The [mother/father] gave undertakings to the court [as set out on the [undertaking form] signed by [her/him] on [date] a copy of which is annexed to this order *or* the [mother/father] gave the following undertakings to the court *[specify]*

9. KEY ISSUES *[only if adjourned]*
The issues which remain to be determined are as follows:-

a)	
b)	
c)	
d)	

Final Order – Child Arrangements Programme

10. After reading the materials provided to the court.

The court heard no oral evidence
or
After hearing the evidence of the following witnesses:-

Name of witness	Called by

THE COURT ORDERS:

11. CHILD ARRANGEMENTS
Such as
- [By consent,] that the arrangements for the children shall be [as set out in the schedule to this order *(if extensive)*/as follows..*[specify]*]
- [a contact warning notice will be endorsed][by consent] that the [father/mother] shall make the child[ren] available to spend time with / have [indirect] contact with] the [father/mother] as set out in the schedule to this order *(if extensive)*/as follows...*[specify]*

12. PARENTAL RESPONSIBILITY
Further to the Child Arrangements Order made *[today/date]*, which provides that the child is to live with [the father, who does not currently have parental responsibility] / [*woman* who is a parent of the child by virtue of section 43 of the Human Fertilisation and Embryology Act 2008, without parental responsibility], the court grants parental responsibility to [the father] / [*the woman*].

Further to the Child Arrangements Order made *[today/date]*, which provides that the child is to spend time or otherwise have contact (but not live) with [the father, who does not currently have parental responsibility] / [*woman* who is a parent of the child by virtue of section 43 of the Human Fertilisation and Embryology Act 2008, without parental responsibility], the court grants parental responsibility to [the father] / [*the woman*].

Further to the Child Arrangements Order made *[today/date]*, which provides that the child is to live with [*a person who is not the parent or guardian of the child concerned is named in the order as a person with whom the child is to spend time or otherwise have contact but not live*] the court grants parental responsibility for the child for as long as the order is in place.

Further to the Child Arrangements Order made *[today/date]*, which provides that the child is to spend time or otherwise have contact (but not live) with [*a person who is not the parent or guardian of the child concerned is named in the order as a person with whom the child is to spend time or otherwise have contact but not live*] the court grants parental responsibility for the child for as long as the order is in place.

Final Order – Child Arrangements Programme

13. ACTIVITY CONDITIONS
[if made at this hearing, specify as appropriate]

Such as:-
The [father/mother] [other party] is directed to take part in:
Set out any order for Activity Direction/Condition [e.g. Separated Parents Information Programme] such dates and times as are specified by.......[the provider]

The court shall forthwith send this order to the provider.

14. PROHIBITED STEPS
Specify as appropriate, such as:-
- The [mother/father] shall not cause or permit [name child[ren] to [cease to attend...*name school*] [live at an address other than *[specify]*] [come into contact with *[specify]*] without the prior written agreement of the [father/mother] or an order of the court.
- The [mother/father] shall not remove [name child/ren] from England and Wales without the prior written agreement of [father/mother] or an order of the court [except ....*[specify]*]

15. SPECIFIC ISSUE - REMOVAL FROM THE JURISDICTION
   (a) The [mother/father] is permitted to remove [name of child(ren)] from England and   Wales on or after [date] to live permanently in [as appropriate]
   (b) *[for example]* Before the removal of the [name child[ren] from the jurisdiction, the   [mother/father] shall obtain, and then deliver and send to the court and to the other parties, an order from [court] an order reflecting the terms of this order insofar as   they relate to the child arrangements [or as appropriate].

16. SPECIFIC ISSUE – SCHOOLING
From [date/the start of the ....term ...] [name child[ren]] shall attend [name and address of school]
[set out any ancillary provisions re schooling e.g. provision of information, fees etc.]

17. SPECIFIC ISSUE – OTHER STEPS
Specify as appropriate

18. CONTACT CENTRE DIRECTION
The order for supported contact at the [   ] contact centre is subject to the following conditions for its operation and effect:-
   a. The [parties/ solicitors for the [Mother/Father][   ] shall inform the centre co-ordinator of the contents of this order as soon s practicable.
   b. The [parties/ solicitors for the parties] shall jointly be responsible for
      i. completing a referral form for the centre co-ordinator and
      ii. providing a copy of this order and any subsisting injunction orders involving the parties to the co-ordinator as soon as practicable and in any event within 2 days of today.
   c. Confirmation from the centre co-ordinator that:
      i. the centre is an accredited member of NACCC;

Final Order – Child Arrangements Programme

        ii. the referral has been accepted following completion of a preparation for contact interview (which interview is a compulsory requirement of all NACCC centres);

        iii. a vacancy is available or the parties have been allocated a place upon a waiting list (the order for supported contact is suspended during any waiting period until a place is available).

  d. The parties and any person permitted to accompany them to the centre shall abide by the rules of the centre.

  e. The parties must attend a preparation for contact meeting with the centre co-ordinator (the parties' solicitors, if acting, must take responsibility for ensuring that information about the meeting is passed to the parties).

  f. The [Mother/Father] [   ]
agrees to take the child(ren) for a pre-contact introductory visit to the centre.

  g. The child(ren) will be informed of the contact arrangements by [Mother/ Father] [   ]

  h. The following arrangements for the contact sessions shall apply:-

        i. The child(ren) shall be taken to the centre by

        ii. The child(ren) shall be collected at the conclusion of contact by

        iii. The [Father/Mother] [   ] may [not] be accompanied during the contact session [by]

        iv. The [Father/Mother] [   ] may [not] remain in the same room as the child(ren) during the contact session

        v. After [   ] sessions of contact, the [Father/Mother] [ ] shall not remain in the same room as the child(ren) but may remain in the confines of the centre.

        vi. [Other agreements about contact at the centre]

  i. The [parties/ the parties' solicitors] shall jointly be responsible for informing the centre co-ordinator when the place is no longer required.

19. MONITORING CONTACT ORDER

(a) Cafcass/CAFCASS Cymru shall, pursuant to s11H Children Act 1989, make an officer available to monitor whether the person required to allow the contact, or the person having contact with the child[ren] complies with the contact order

(b) The contact monitoring order shall remain in force until [   ] [up to 12 mths]

(c) The [mother / father / person having contact] shall co-operate with the Cafcass officer / WFPO [in particular by ….] so that the officer can comply with the order to monitor the contact;

(d) The Cafcass officer / WFPO is directed to prepare a report for the Court (and provide a copy to the parties) if he/she considers that the order is not being complied with; the report shall include any information which the Cafcass officer / WFPO considers relevant to the issue of compliance and shall specifically advise on the question of whether the order should be varied or discharged.

20. FAMILY ASSISTANCE ORDER

(a) Cafcass/CAFCASS Cymru/[   ] Local Authority shall, pursuant to s16 Children Act 1989, make an Officer available to advise assist and (where

Final Order – Child Arrangements Programme

appropriate) befriend the following persons who have (save for a named child) today consented to the making of this Order:

    a.

(b) The Family Assistance Order shall remain in force until [   ]_[up to 12 mths]

(c) The Officer is directed to give advice and assistance as regards establishing, improving and maintaining contact to those identified above

(d) The Officer is directed to report to the Court by 16:00hs on [   ] on the following matters (*including but limited to the question of whether the s8 order should be varied or discharged*):

    a.

(e) It is recorded for the purpose of this Order that

        a. the opinion of the appropriate officer has been obtained and

        b. all relevant persons have been given the opportunity to comment on that opinion prior to the making of this order pursuant to PD12M FPR 2010

(f) The Local Authority/Cafcass/CAFCASS Cymru may send representations to the Court and the other parties on or before [14 days from service] as to the making of the Family Assistance Order pursuant to PD12M FPR 2010. Any party wishing to respond to those representations must do so within 7 days of receipt.

21. COSTS

No order as to costs *or*

Costs in the application *or*

Costs reserved *or*

Funded services assessment of the costs of *[specify] or*

Other *[specify]*

Dated

Court address: for sending documents/communication:

Appendix 2: Child Arrangements Programme Flowchart

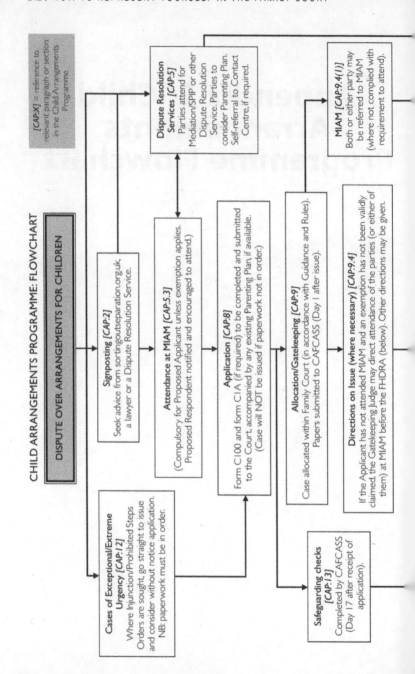

CHILD ARRANGEMENTS PROGRAMME: FLOWCHART

DISPUTE OVER ARRANGEMENTS FOR CHILDREN

[CAPX] = reference to relevant paragraph or section in the Child Arrangements Programme

Cases of Exceptional/Extreme Urgency [CAP:12]
Where Injunction/Prohibited Steps Orders are sought, go straight to issue and consider without notice application. NB: paperwork must be in order.

Signposting [CAP:2]
Seek advice from sortingoutseparation.org.uk, a lawyer or a Dispute Resolution Service.

Dispute Resolution Services [CAP:5]
Parties attend for Mediation/SPIP or other Dispute Resolution Service. Parties to consider Parenting Plan. Self-referral to Contact Centre, if required.

Attendance at MIAM [CAP:5.3]
(Compulsory for Proposed Applicant unless exemption applies. Proposed Respondent notified and encouraged to attend.)

MIAM [CAP:9.4(I)]
Both or either party may be referred to MIAM (where not complied with requirement to attend).

Application [CAP:8]
Form C100 and form C1A (if required) to be completed and submitted to the Court, accompanied by any existing Parenting Plan, if available. (Case will NOT be issued if paperwork not in order.)

Safeguarding checks [CAP:13]
Completed by CAFCASS (Day 17 after receipt of application).

Allocation/Gatekeeping [CAP:9]
Case allocated within Family Court (in accordance with Guidance and Rules). Papers submitted to CAFCASS (Day I after issue).

Directions on Issue (where necessary) [CAP:9.4]
If the Applicant has not attended MIAM and an exemption has not been validly claimed, the Gatekeeping Judge may direct attendance of the parties (or either of them) at MIAM before the FHDRA (below). Other directions may be given.

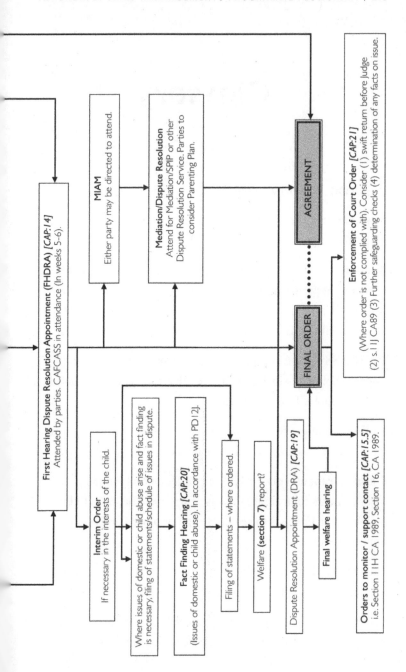

First Hearing Dispute Resolution Appointment (FHDRA) *[CAP:14]*
Attended by parties. CAFCASS in attendance (In weeks 5–6).

MIAM
Either party may be directed to attend.

Mediation/Dispute Resolution
Attend for Mediation/SPIP or other Dispute Resolution Service. Parties to consider Parenting Plan.

AGREEMENT

FINAL ORDER

Enforcement of Court Order *[CAP:21]*
(Where order is not complied with). Consider (1) swift return before Judge (2) s.11J CA89 (3) Further safeguarding checks (4) determination of any facts on issue.

Interim Order
If necessary in the interests of the child.

Where issues of domestic or child abuse arise and fact finding is necessary, filing of statements/schedule of issues in dispute.

Fact Finding Hearing *[CAP:20]*
(Issues of domestic or child abuse). In accordance with PD 12J.

Filing of statements – where ordered.

Welfare (section 7) report?

Dispute Resolution Appointment (DRA) *[CAP:19]*

Final welfare hearing

Orders to monitor / support contact *[CAP:15.5]*
i.e. Section 11H CA 1989, Section 16, CA 1989.

Glossary

Applicant – the person applying for a particular Order.

Application – the way you begin court proceedings, or ask for particular to be taken in your case.

Barrister – a self-employed legal professional whose job it is to represent parties at particular court hearings. They can be instructed by Solicitors to conduct particular hearings, or Direct Access qualified Barristers can be instructed by the public directly.

CAFCASS – the Children and Family Courts Advisory and Support Service, which is an agency that can become involved and prepare reports for children cases.

Child – usually refers to a person under 18 but it is very unusual to have Orders made about children aged over 16.

Child Arrangements Order – an Order setting out the arrangements for a child in terms of whom he or she is to live with, and when he or she is to see the parent or other family members applying for Orders.

Consent Order – where the parties reach an agreement as to the way forward and an Order is prepared for the Court to consider.

Contact – where a person spends some time with a child. This is now also referred to as spending time with a child.

Directions Hearing – a hearing in which the Court sets out the steps needed to decide an application.

Facts and Reasons – the equivalent of a judgment in the Magistrates Court.

Family Court – The Court that has the jurisdiction to make Orders about children. This is used to refer to all levels of Judge in the Family Court.

FHDRA – First Hearing and Dispute Resolution Appointment. This is an important hearing in any application for an Order about a child. It is used to set out what steps are to be taken to decide the application

Final Hearing – the hearing where final decisions are made.

Findings of Fact – decisions the Court has made after hearing evidence. These findings can include whether a person lied, whether a person is being unreasonable and whether a person was violent.

Findings of Fact/Split hearing – a hearing set up to decide particular issues of fact before a final decision is made.

Guardian – a professional, often a CAFCASS officer, who can be appointed at the same time as a Solicitor for the child, whose job it is to act in that child's interests in court.

Human Rights – the Court has to take into account the fundamental rights of the parties. This includes the right to a fair trial and a right to a private life. Where the rights of the parents and the child are not compatible, the child's rights are more important.

Indirect Contact – contact between a parent and child, which does not involve direct communication. This usually takes the form of letters, cards and gifts.

Interim Hearing – the hearing where decisions are made on short-term issues which are not agreed but need to be decided before a Final Hearing.

Judgment – the Court's decision. This is not just the Court Order. It includes the reasons an Order is being made, and whether anyone was not telling the truth.

Leave – permission (where permission is needed) for a party to apply for an Order.

Local Authority – another way of referring to Social Services. Also sometimes referred to as Children's Services.

McKenzie Friend – a non-lawyer who can assist you in court behind the scenes. They can be allowed to ask questions on your behalf in court if the Judge allows it.

Mediation Information and Assessment Meeting (MIAM) – an appointment with a mediator to consider whether the dispute over the child can be resolved by agreement without the need for court proceedings.

No Order Principle – the principle that the Court should not make an Order unless it is better to do that than make no Order at all.

Notice – the amount of warning given to another party before an application is made. Some urgent hearings can be without notice; other applications need a set amount of time to be given.

Parental Responsibility – the rights and responsibilities of being a parent. This includes the right to consent to medical treatment and the right to information about a child.

Parties – the people who are 'party' to the court proceedings, namely the person making the application and the person responding to it. There can be more than one applicant or respondent.

Penal Notice – a Notice written on a Court Order that explains that any person breaking that part of the Order without reasonable excuse can be imprisoned or fined.

Position Statement – a document where you set out your case on particular issues, usually those identified by the Judge. This might include your proposals for contact, or whether you think the Court should order a Finding of Fact Hearing.

Practice Direction – guidance given by a senior Judge about aspects of children cases.

Respondent – the person applying for a particular Order.

Return Date – when a Court makes an Order without notice to the other party, it must set a date to allow the person who didn't have notice to come and set out their side of the story.

Scott Schedule – a table of allegations that the Court is asked to decide. A Scott Schedule will set out both the allegation made and the party's response.

Section 7 Report – the report ordered under Section 7 of the Children Act on issues such as contact and residence. Also called a CAFCASS report if it is to be written by a CAFCASS officer. It can also be written by Social Services.

Section 37 Report – a more serious report, asking Social Services to investigate an issue of child protection.

Service – the process of giving notice to the other party of your application. This can include personal service (arranging for Notice of the Application to be given to the other side in person, usually through a process server) or postal service to the last known address.

Shared Care – where the care of the child is shared between the parents. This does not have to mean an equal division of time.

Skeleton argument – similar to a position statement but written to set out your case on complicated issues, often by referring to the law.

Solicitor for the Child – where the Court has decided that the child or children concerned should be legally represented, a Solicitor will be appointed to act for the child.

Statement of Service – a statement confirming that a person was served, and by what means.

Substituted Service – where the Court allows a person to be served using a different method to the one ordinarily required.

Supervised Contact – usually used to refer to contact which is fully supervised by professionals at a Contact Centre but in some cases extended family members can also be permitted to do this.

Supported Contact – usually refers to a more loose form of supervision. In this situation, the supervisor is much less involved but keeps an overall eye on proceedings.

Warning Notice – a Notice written on an Order that explains that anyone not making the child available to see the other parent in line with the Court Order without reasonable excuse can be punished, to include imprisonment or a fine.

Welfare Principle – the key principle in deciding any children case, namely that the welfare of the child is the paramount consideration.

Witness Statement – a statement, supported by a statement confirming it is true, in which a person sets out their case, or gives their version of events in writing.

Welfare Checklist – a list of considerations the Court needs to take into account when deciding certain applications.

Index